Praise For

"As a reporter and I.
of poor choices, discouragement, and disaster. In *Rich People Shop Here*, the story of Patsy and Boots reminds us that no challenge can extinguish hope. No hardship can separate you from the Author of that hope, your loving Father, Who will never fail you. Read this, and be encouraged to take one more step! Just like rich people."

-Carolyn Castleberry, CBN News Reporter and Author of *It's About Time and Women, Take Charge of Your Money.*

"*Rich People Shop Here* is the gripping account of one woman's long and desperate struggle with hardship and misfortune. It is at the same time a testimony to the power of faith and healing in redirecting a person's life. It is a story of ultimate triumph and hope."

-George Gallup, JR.

"I love this story! *Rich People Shop Here* is an amazing but true-to- life Power of WHO story. Patsy's 'WHO' came to her aide and helped her forever change the trajectory of her life. In the same way she teaches us how to be 'Moment Makers' for our friends and family."

-Bob Beaudine, Bestselling Author, *The Power of WHO*

Rich People Shop Here is inspiring and well-written and I believe it has the same kind of broad appeal and potential as Tuesdays with Morrie or Annie Lamott. Oh, and amid all that was going on with Patsy, there's a lot of fun and funny moments that make this a terrific read.

-Barbara Cave Henricks, CEO and President of Cave Henricks Communications.

Rich PEOPLE SHOP HERE

A Tale of Love, Redemption, and Bargain Hunting

Dennis Welch

aBM

RICH PEOPLE SHOP HERE

Published by:

A Book's Mind

PO Box 272847

Fort Collins, CO 80527

www.abooksmind.com

ISBN 978-1-939828-87-3

Copyright © 2010 by Dennis Welch

Second Edition 2014

Printed in the United States of America

TABLE OF CONTENTS

Foreword-George Gallup   I

Introduction   III

Chapter 1: A Pre-funeral Celebration   1

A Patsy Moment - Blackmailing the Kids   11

Chapter 2: Moving Around   17

Chapter 3: Harbingers   27

A Patsy Moment - The Rod and Reel Toss   33

Chapter 4: Love and Marriage(s)   37

Chapter 5: Fun and Frog #2   43

A Patsy Moment - "Yonder Goes Your Momma"   50

Chapter 6: "Dude"   53

Chapter 7: Wedded Bliss   63

A Patsy Moment - "I See Deaf People"   68

Chapter 8: Redemption   71

A Patsy Moment - The Wizard of Oddities   87

Chapter 9: Brothers and Bullets-Living on Deerfield Street   91

Chapter 10: Healing   119

Chapter 11: Missions of Mercy   125

A Patsy Moment: Delivering the Avon   136

Chapter 12: The Lion Sleeps   139

A Ron Moment - Driver's Education   152

Chapter 13: Nuclei   157

A Patsy Moment - Driving Miss Patsy   174

Chapter 14: Tanners to the Rescue   177

Chapter 15: Testify   187

This is dedicated to all of the great women in my life- Susie, my wife; Patsy, my mother; Ollie Bell, my grandmother; and too many others to mention by name. My life is richer because you cared.Dennis

FOREWORD

Rich People Shop Here is the gripping account of one woman's long and desperate struggle with hardship and misfortune, a true testimony to the power of faith and healing in redirecting a person's life. It is a story of ultimate triumph and hope.

While each of us faces the inevitable vicissitudes and trials of life, Patsy bore more pain and heartache than most. Abandoned by her mother at a very early age, Patsy began a search for stability and home. At the tender age of fourteen, she married for the first time. Not only did she not find stability, she stumbled into calamities for which she was wholly unprepared: unstable and alcoholic husbands who left her for periods of time; hospitalizations and sickness; and times of desperate poverty.

This book is filled with valuable insights and lessons for how to have a better life. Dennis reminds readers of the importance of having a "special" person in our lives (in addition to a spouse or partner), who is a true friend, constant companion, and a person in whom one can confide and who holds us accountable. For Patsy, that person was "Boots", whom she met in 1953. And for the past forty years or so Patsy and Boots have taken calls at all times during day and night from other people in trouble, people just like them who are looking to change the trajectory of their lives and just need to know

I

how. Their lives and work together have made a real difference, and both women would agree that their coming together was no mere coincidence.

Dennis Welch writes in an easy and entertaining style. He has a sharp eye for the humorous, the bizarre, and the unconventional. He sprinkles this compelling tale with lighthearted breaks he calls "Patsy Moments"…fun and funny snapshots that reveal Patsy's unique (and endearing) characteristics and misadventures.

Most of all, though, ***Rich People Shop Here*** is a story that returns over and over again to a simple but vitally important theme: *No matter where you are in life, better days are ahead.* Readers of this book, who, like the rest of us, sometimes feel overwhelmed by life, will draw deep inspiration and encouragement from ***Rich People Shop Here***.

By the late George Gallup, Jr. and his wife, the late Kingsley Gallup

INTRODUCTION

In a sometimes cynical world it is easy to believe that there are no happy endings; that most people who struggle to get somewhere never actually get there, that the notion of any of us rising above our circumstances and upbringing is a notion for Pollyannas and people who are mostly out of touch with reality.

Nothing could be further from the truth, and the story you are about to read is living proof of that. Take heart. There is still romance, mercy, salvation, resurrection, and laughter- all available and in ample supply. No one is so far down that they cannot drink from the cup that contains those all-important ingredients of the good life. Let me encourage you: no matter where you are today in your walk through this world, the potential for you to have a life well-lived is still within your grasp. Trust me.

It has always been my contention that the closer one comes to escaping one's circumstances the louder the chorus of failure gets. It whispers in your ear every day when you're defeated and not trying. Take just a few concrete steps toward a better life and the decibels really begin to rise. Near the exit, the noise is deafening. "Look at your upbringing" it says. Or, "you're not worth it," or "this won't work" or "this will be another one of your temporary fixes." We've all heard it from time to time.

And oftentimes the cacophony brings company. Miserable people enjoy congregating with other miserable people and reassuring each other that they are all ok. Or even worse, that they are not all ok, but that it's not their fault. The talk at these gatherings usually includes at least a portion of the time being spent railing on "my circumstances, my bad luck, the government, my parents, somebody who done me wrong," all or some of these conspiring to hold them back from being all that they could be. I suppose there's some kind of comfort here, where everybody's life is in the pits. Many people live their entire existence on this earth and never break free from these paralyzing surroundings, often dying penniless, broken, and in denial. Some, though, miraculously get a momentary glimpse of another kind of life. Many times the admonition to step out and step up comes from just one true friend who cares deeply for them and is willing to get on their horse and ride in and save them despite the slings and arrows associated with doing so.

It's an age old story, really. Someone with hope shows up. Arriving at a better life more often than not requires great sacrifice and perhaps even separation. Most importantly, though, we need to hear the good news that someone else has escaped, and that they accomplished it even though they share many if not all of our weaknesses and shortcomings.

I hope this tale does that for you. It's a very encouraging and completely true story. It has it all, really. Poverty, abandonment, alcoholism, drug addiction, divorce, jail-you name it, it's here somewhere.

You or someone you know may be dealing with all or some of these issues. In reality every family does, though many don't talk about it or acknowledge it. One thing for certain: the problems will surely linger as long as they are ignored. Fixing them absolutely requires facing them.

You may finally be nearing your exit from the difficult life you've always lived and you may be seeking something better because you just know in your heart it's there and you are willing to do anything to find it.

My advice to you? For the time it takes for you to read this story, tune out the world, your relatives, your in-laws, your parents, your teachers- whoever it is that has told you that you *can't escape*.

Because, they are wrong.

You *can*.

Boots & Patsy, circa 2000

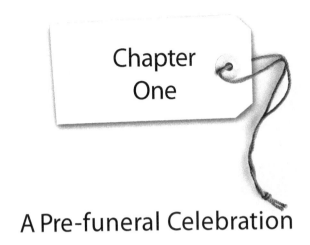

Chapter One

A Pre-funeral Celebration

A good name is better than silver.

Proverbs

Sometimes the chasm between where we are and where we would like to be seems vast and unable to be spanned no matter how hard we try. Our better future lingers off in the mist, distant and shadowy. Grasping it requires a mix of faith, perseverance, hard work and obedience.

As she sat on the wooden bench in her white luminescent car hop outfit and surveyed the parking lot filled with cars, friends, and customers, a faint smile crossed Patsy Yates' tired but still beautiful face. For just a moment she thought she got a glimpse of where she was going, and it comforted her a bit.

If only she had known on that muggy Houston night back in 1953 that someday…

Surprise!

There are two constants about Patsy, my mother. One, she has kind of weird Lucille Ball types of episodes and if you're going to hang out with her you'll probably have to participate. Over her life she has had driving episodes, leaving her children episodes (accidentally, she claims), miraculous unexplainable episodes, and generally odd but true episodes. She has a good time with all of it, and the people who are in her orbit fully expect her to do this stuff. The episodes live in legend in the Welch family, and like old sitcoms, are rerun often over Thanksgiving dinner, Christmas get-togethers, etc.

Secondly, she has always had great friends. Throughout her life she has obeyed the admonition that if one is to have friends they must show themselves friendly. She certainly did that. So, it came as no surprise, really, when on a cold Sunday afternoon back in 2000, two good friends of the Welch family, Pauline Johnston and Gaye Johns, called my house to discuss the possibility and the logistics of putting on a "pre-funeral celebration" for my Mom (Patsy) and her lifelong friend, Boots Jackson. The Johnstons (David and Pauline) and The Johns (Roy and Gaye) are two of Mom's and Boots' best friends from the 60's. David was my first Sunday school teacher that I can remember. I don't recall all the lessons that he taught, but I do remember that he was always there and that he was kind to a bunch of smart-aleck eight-year- old boys. He and Pauline are two of those really good-hearted people who work hard, and they are generous to a fault. They have done well in this life on every front and they deserve everything they have earned, including their circle of lifelong friends. The Johns' were missionaries to Peru and Brother Roy pastored our church for awhile when they were home on sabbatical. Great people, all, with good hearts and generous souls. If they love you, you know it. So, their desire to honor Mom and Boots was not surprising, really.

Good Cop, Bad Cop

I chuckle a little when I think about these two women they wanted to honor. Boots Jackson and Patsy Welch could not be more different.

Boots is a swarthy, loud, dramatic person who is more fun than she has a right to be. She doesn't mince words ever, so if you come to her for advice you had better be prepared to get it straight on, right between the eyes. And, she really likes for you to do something about it after the talk. Action. She likes action and excitement. She is very public and outspoken. No secrets.

Patsy is private and tactful. She can talk the horns off a billy goat but she is more genteel in her counsel. Yes, she is always happy to talk with you if you really need help. Yes, she would like for you to do what she suggests, but she would never wrestle you to the ground and pin you until you cried "Uncle!" and acquiesced and changed your life.

Boots would.

Once, Boots was in charge of the youth department at our church and none of the youth could keep up with her. She could stay up all night, work all day, and do it all over again the next night. There were lots of parties that ran late into the night. No drinking, no drugs, just good clean fun, non-stop. One night a young man named Rick Shrader was at one of these fiestas and he had no idea what was about to happen to him. He had visited the church a few times, mainly (by his own admission) because of the cute girls who attended there. On this night, Boots grabbed him by his shirtsleeve and took him into one of her rooms at her house and closed the door, bracing it shut with her foot. Her basso voice boomed over the sound of music blaring from the living room: "Rick, just because you are in a garage doesn't mean you're a car. Right? Then, coming to church doesn't make you a Christian, either. You've been hanging out at this church for awhile now. It's time you accepted Jesus as your savior. Let's pray." He did, and for the past 30 years he has been the pastor of a great church in Katy, Texas that has done some of the most charitable work in his area, feeding the hungry, and reaching out to the homeless. Great work that is changing the world he lives in. Probably not exactly the way the Apostle Paul would have done it (or maybe exactly how he would have done it, given all we know about him), but Boots has her own methods: she pinned him, and the world is better for it.

Patsy would never even think to do that. But that doesn't mean she doesn't have any idiosyncrasies. Once, my dad was asked if he ever watched Lucille Ball. "Watch her?" he said, "I live with her." She's always gotten lost a lot and she's done weird things with her cars. Her synapses fire funny and occasionally she does things that are completely inexplicable. And yet, she can teach the Bible for two hours with no notes of any kind. It has always been miraculous, really, to hear her speak, especially if you were one of her young sons who she left at the grocery store only the day before.

Somehow, these two very different people were a team, the EMT of counselors, if you will. They got calls at all hours from desperate people and for more than 40 years they had responded with no regard for themselves, their time, their lives, the dangers that may lurk, nothing. They were always there, oftentimes together, to rescue the perishing. "Good cop, Bad cop" is what one rescued soul called them: Mom, sweetly chiding and encouraging, Boots breathing fire and brimstone, both doing so with a lot of love and concern.

4

Everybody knew that. That's why Pauline and Gaye were calling me to put together this shindig.

"We shouldn't wait until people die to tell them what we think of them should we?" Pauline asked me, rhetorically. "Of course we shouldn't," I responded not really sure where the conversation was going.

"Then, let's have a big pre-funeral celebration for your mom and Boots. It will be fun."

Indeed it would be. This group definitely knew how to do that. I listened intently as they unfolded the scenario for how it might come to pass.

Filling the Room

The premise was simple; we would enlist a few of this duo's inner circle of friends and allies to build a list of potential invitees. Then, on the sly, we would secretly invite a few hundred of Mom's and Boots' closest friends to join us at Mom's church to celebrate their lives and the 40 years or so of work they had been doing all (or at least most) of their adult lives. Everyone (even those who could not attend) would be asked to write a letter to put into a scrapbook. This letter would be a testimonial about what Mom's and Boot's lives had meant to them with a word of thanks for being obedient to their calling.

Also, any humorous tales about Boots and Patsy would be included in the letters. I wondered how big the scrapbook was going to be. It was going to have to be pretty large to have enough room for all the funny stories because there were so many of them. These two had done it all over the years and even in the direst of circumstances there was always something humorous (either intentional or unintentional) going on. I have chosen just a few that sort of "live in legend" and that I am most familiar with and included them in this book. In fact, every few pages will include a "Patsy Moment." I will have to be selective about which of those stories to include or this book will be as thick as *War and Peace*.

But, I digress. Let me get back to the "funeral" arrangements.

Those who were indeed able to attend the event in person would be given the opportunity to speak directly to the two guests of honor from the stage about how their work impacted their lives and the lives of their families and those around them.

The most difficult part of this whole deal would be keeping the secret. After more than three decades of friendship the vine that connected this group was advanced beyond anything that man has ever invented. Everybody knew everybody else's business in a good kind of way because they really cared for each other. The bond between them that began all those years ago at Thornton Street Baptist Church was as strong as ever and they talked among themselves on at least a weekly basis.

We remained hopeful about being able to successfully invite 400 people to a Saturday morning event in a little fellowship hall at Airline United Methodist Church in Houston, Texas. The invitation letters were sent and we held our breath, hoping people would respond in one way or another.

"Funeral" Day

The morning of the big day arrived and we were all set. The scrapbook was packed to overflowing with many RSVP's and letters from literally all over the world, each with accolades and anecdotes about these two great women. The parking lot began to fill up and soon the room was filled to capacity with well wishers and friends. At last, the guests of honor arrived and were so surprised by the whole thing that I was actually afraid for just a fleeting moment that it was going to be too much for them. But, soon they both recovered and the show got underway.

All morning long, hour after hour, one person after another came up to the microphone and began to recount how they had met Boots and Mom and what their circumstances had been at the time they met. Many had been in dire straits, at their wits end, strung out on drugs or alcohol, homeless or penniless. One lady had lived next door to us with her alcoholic husband, and one day she banged on our front door frantically, and screamed for us to "hurry and open the door!!!" When we opened the door, she was practically naked, wearing only a slip and covering her upper body with a towel. It turned out that her husband, Chuck, in a fit of drunken rage, had piled all of her clothes in to a heap in the front yard and burned them up. She was clothes-less. We took her and her young son in for a few days until her husband settled down enough for her to go back home. She hid out with us. More about this later.

We always had a lot of drama like that around our house. One time, I came home from school and upon reaching my front porch, I was pulled into the door by my mother yelling "hurry, get down, the people two doors down have been shooting at each other!" One of them (the husband) was eventually shot in the stomach by his irate and slightly deranged wife. He lived, but his ever present limp always reminded me of that afternoon.

All of these people, and many, many others, wound up going to church with us and finding a different life there for themselves. Many of them, at least the ones who were still alive, were there on this special day and delighted in telling their stories. There was a lot of laughter and tears, skits and stories, hugs and handshakes. As the day came to an end I sat alone in the now empty hall and pondered the whole thing. Isn't this how every person wants to be remembered? Doesn't everyone want to get to the end of their life and still have a great reputation and be revered and honored?

I would certainly think so.

An outsider might have wondered what could have brought such an outpouring of affection on two seemingly regular folks. They had never climbed Mt. Everest, never built a skyscraper, or run for office. They weren't scientists or Harvard grads.

But they did have one important thing in common. They were givers-of their time, corn dogs (I'll explain later), talents, and yes, money (if they really thought you needed it).

A Boat and a Car, Maybe

Yes, if you really needed money even that could be arranged. As a young boy I was surprised when I would see Mom give away money. Most of the time she was so tight with the family funds that I thought at the time we must be saving it all for something really big. Actually, even though her bank account stayed the same most of the time, Mom would waver back and forth between feeling incredibly wealthy and completely destitute.

"I'm thinking about buying your daddy a boat and a new truck to pull it with" she would say out of the blue in a wealthy-feeling moment. I would seize upon these moments to ask if I might have a dime to buy a coke. (Yes, you could buy a coke with just ten cents back then. It was a long time ago.) It seemed like the opportune time, especially with boats and new trucks coming into view on the family's financial horizon.

"What do you think I am, made out of money?" she'd shout. Uh, well, no. I guess not now. Under my breath I would mutter something about how if cokes were outside the budgetary constraints, then boats and trucks were probably not going to happen anytime soon either.

Somehow we got by, though. Once, when my dad and uncles were in business together (the short-lived Welch Brothers Machine shop), my dad brought home much less than the poverty level for several years, and yet we had all we needed and we never missed a meal or went without clothes, or school supplies. I distinctly remember many mornings before school, we would pray for food and our daily bread, so to speak. We always had it by the day's end.

In those days she would take me to thrift stores over in what I considered the seedy parts of town to buy school clothes. "Don't worry boys, rich people shop here" she would always say preemptively to us as we got out of the car and headed inside. Occasionally we would have to step over a couple of the wealthiest ones who had passed out in the doorway of the establishment. "That must have been the Rockefeller's" I wisecracked once, but she pretended not to listen.

She was on a mission and she would not be deterred or discouraged. Taking care of her family was really her life's work and this was part of it. With all Patsy had been through in her life, shopping in a second hand store for hand-me-down clothes was no big deal. Her pride never got in the way of what really mattered.

And did she mean it when she said that rich people shop at those thrift stores in the "seedy" part of town? I suppose it depends on your definition of wealth. If being wealthy means having friends and people who love you unconditionally, and a reputation in your old age that shines like gold, than she was right. Rich people did shop there, and she seems to be getting richer by the day.

But, the truth is, there was a day when she and Boots were not so rich. They were just two warriors on the ropes and barely standing.

I would imagine that the last thing either of them would have thought at that time was that one day they would be loved so and respected even more. Thick and ominous clouds hung heavy over their lives back then that seemed destined to do them in.

If a day like this celebration day was ever going to happen, somehow, the rescuers would need to be rescued.

A Patsy Moment - Blackmailing the Kids

When we were young boys, my dad was a machinist and sometimes he would work the second shift, from 2:30-10:30 PM. That, unfortunately, meant that on those evenings he wouldn't be home for supper. We all liked having him home for supper, but my mom especially did. His presence always insured peace and tranquility in the home, mainly because he maintained an austere and commanding presence. Nobody tested him. Nobody. Most remarkably, he was able to pull that off without raising his voice, or throwing fits, or anything. He just had it. Later, when I watched my first Clint Eastwood spaghetti western I realized "hey, I know this character. He's the guy that looks over my report card every six weeks." The only thing missing was the poncho and the cigarillo.

Anyway, when he wasn't around, it was pandemonium. Dinner was a circus. My brothers and I would throw food, fight with each other, and argue. You name it, we did it. Mom would try to corral us, but alas it was to no avail. We were 7, 12, and 17.

"Pass the bread!!!!" my brother shouted as if we were all hard of hearing. I grabbed the loaf and dropped back in the pocket, surveying the field to find an open receiver. Then, I flung the bread across the table and hit my brother squarely in the face, setting off a wrestling match on the floor, which I lost in three falls as I recall.

This went on night after night.

On one particularly memorable night, mom wasn't acting like herself at all. We boys fired up the dinnertime party and she just sat and minded her own business and ate her food and kept to herself.

No yelling or threatening. Nothing. We thought she might be sick or something.

We "passed" the bread, stuck our fingers in each other's mashed potatoes, wrestled and screamed, and just generally made complete fools of ourselves.

After about 30 minutes or so, she interrupted our little shindig: "You boys done?" she asked. I popped off "Done? Yeah, we're done, we're well done, just like this steak." I distinctly recall exactly what I said at that moment because of what happened next.

Mother got very calm, and she reached across the table into the flower pot that was the dinner table's centerpiece. She pulled out a little microphone and then she opened the oven and took out a reel to reel tape recorder. Everything was moving in slow motion, now. The buttons on that little cheap tape recorder sounded like cannons going off as she stopped the tape and rewound to the beginning. She smiled a sinister smile while she played back the entire dinner episode to us. Our behinds tingled thinking about what "The man with no name" would do to us when he heard this stuff. Oh, boy.

We dropped to our knees and begged for clemency, and hoped that the milk of human kindness still flowed. After a prolonged period of sobbing and sucking up she finally relented. Not without some conditions, however.

"Now," she said her voice lowering into a scary register like mafia guys sound when they're about to make you an offer you can't (and shouldn't) refuse.

"I'll tell you what I'm going to do." She was boxing up the tape and putting it into her blouse pocket with a safecracker's dexterity and smoothness. We three sat in rapt silence. I can't imagine what our faces must have looked like at that moment. We hung on her every word.

"I'm going to hide this tape in a place that only I know about." Then, she gave the terms for this undeserved act of mercy. "I won't play it for your father as long as I get co-operation from you three." Brando would have been proud of this performance had he been aware of the drama transpiring that night at the Deerfield Street Theatre.

Wow. *Blackmail*, I thought. Our mother has resorted to blackmail. Are we that evil that we've driven her to this?

For years when things would begin to get out of hand she would get eerily calm, her hand raised toward us, index finger pointing skyward, "Don't forget THE TAPE." We surely didn't, and no matter where we were thinking of going, behaviorally speaking, order was immediately restored.

On my high school graduation night mom came to me, crestfallen and obviously heavy hearted about something. "I need to confess something to you, son."

Okay, Momma, Fire away.

"You remember that tape I threatened you boys with all those years?" "Of course, mother, how could I forget?"

"Well, I want you to know that I threw it away the next day after I recorded it. I felt horrible about taping you guys without you knowing it and blackmailing you, so my conscience wouldn't let me keep the tape."

Hmmm. I pointed out to her that apparently her conscience had not been piqued enough to keep her from still leveraging the tape through the years to keep calm in the house when she needed it. So, blackmail is bad but fibbing isn't?

Apparently not, if your motives are pure.

I did forgive her and we had a good laugh about it back there in 1974, standing in the Houston Coliseum among all the other proud graduates and their parents. The story has been told plenty of times down through the years. It is one of the pieces of "Patsy-ology" that people want to hear over and over again. I couldn't blame her a bit for what she did. It was probably an act of desperation. If I had three kids like me and my brothers I would have probably resorted to the same kind of stuff and I wouldn't have been near as nice about it. What she did must have worked on some level. We all grew up and turned out okay for the most part.

The moral of this story for you parents out there who may be reading this?

Whatever works.

Patsy & June Yates, circa early 30's

Annie Laurie & Patsy Yates

Mack & Patsy Yates

1931

Chapter Two

Moving Around

My home, it is my retreat and resting place from wars.
I try to keep this corner as a haven against the tempest
outside, as I do another corner of my soul.

Michel Eyquem De Montaigne

Everybody thinks they know their family stories. I always thought I did until I started this little project. Every Saturday for six months, Mom and I would get together at the breakfast bar in her kitchen and we would turn on the tape recorder to capture the next phase of her life. It never failed. At least once or twice during her discourse I would say "I didn't know that." At first, the exercise was a bit of a chore, but after the first two or three, I began to really look forward to these visits. I began to understand why her and dad's story drew people to them, and why our house was always filled with individuals looking for answers and help, and why even today, Mom's phone rings often with a scared voice on the other end looking for answers.

This exercise is among the most interesting (fascinating, actually) things I have ever done, and one of the many surprises I got was that I learned almost as much about myself as about my mom and dad and their lives, family and friends. I heard some of my own reactions in her stories...my own fears and shortcomings. It turns out that my synapses fire like hers sometimes. More often, they fire like my dad's. I learned that unfortunately, like every human who walks the earth, I got the good and the bad from both sides. It was good to hear that I came by these things honestly, through the bloodline and the DNA and that overcoming the worst of my issues was possible. They had both done it. Despite my dad's sordid past before he was 30 (tremendous battles with alcoholism and many brushes with the law), his last 20 years or so were as good as it gets. On his deathbed he told me in response to my question about how he felt about what he was going through, that he believed that he had been given "a 25 year reprieve." "Someone should have killed me before I made 25," he said in his weakened state. "I got to have a great wife, a great life, and meet my grandkids." At his funeral every seat was taken and people jammed into the chapel and stood shoulder to shoulder around the walls. The reverence for the man was obviously off the scale. Mom, too, is revered and loved more than she knows. Spend just a few minutes with her friends, associates, Bible study students, and family and you'll see what I'm talking about. I don't want to give anything away, but I will tell you that this story has a happy ending. As well it should.

But it certainly didn't begin that way.

Orange, Texas

As you enter Texas from Louisiana on I-10 you encounter a most unusual sign. It says:

Orange, Texas---30 miles

El Paso, Texas---857 Miles.

I always ask myself the same question when I see that sign: Why do I need to know that El Paso is over 800 miles away? It seems a little like bragging to put a sign like that up by the highway, just because you can.

El Paso is a nice place, by the way, but Orange is really special. That's where Patsy Yates was born.

Patsy was born on November 1, 1929 on Bradford Street to Annie Laurie and Mack Yates, two sharp looking, dapper souls. Mack was a projectionist at the local theatre and according to family members always had a job even during the darkest hours of The Great Depression. Annie Laurie was a housewife, but deep in her heart, she longed for more. In retrospect, I'm not sure she ever found it. She would eventually take a job as a timekeeper in the Orange, Texas Shipyards and she would sing in the shipyard band at night. All of the pictures I've ever seen of Mack as a young man showed him to be a sharp dresser with a nice car and snappy clothes. But, his veneer of success hid a dark disease that would begin to surface sometime after Patsy was born. He was an alcoholic.

Annie Laurie was pretty and smart. She and Mack had two other children, Malcolm Vernon (Sonny) and Diana June. By her 4th birthday, Diana June fell ill to pneumonia and like many of the children of that era when medical care was not readily available or as advanced as it is today, she died. Mack and Anne Laurie fought a lot and by the end of the 1930's they were divorced. Anne Laurie spent the months after the divorce living apart from Mac and the kids while working and saving up as much money as she could. Then, with very little warning, she packed up her things and moved to California.

19

She took Sonny with her, but left Patsy behind to begin an extended period of moving and instability.

We all make choices based on what we think will make us happy. Many times these life-altering decisions are made with limited information, a lack of maturity or counsel, and under more duress than we need. Then, after the decision is made and there is no chance to go back, we oftentimes realize that we have erred and we are faced with the challenge of making the most of a bad situation. We may survive these misadventures, but we shouldn't underestimate the damage that each one does to our soul. I've heard Anne Laurie's story many times about how she moved to California and made a lot of money and saved it all. In all the times I've heard it I have never once heard a single word about a joyful life, one that others would envy.

TB, La Cucaracha, and Liberty

"I can't remember much about those first nine years of my life," says Patsy. "They're a blank." I'm no psychologist, but I would guess that she was traumatized by her mother abandoning her and the insecurity of what happened afterwards. Her first memories are of her time spent in the third grade. She had a very high IQ and made good grades in school. "I can't remember the exact number," she says, "but I recall that people talked about the mid 140's."

She liked school a lot and apparently was a fine student. Patsy: "My teacher in the third grade was Mrs. Patricia Long. When she found out my mother had left me she asked if she could have me. I guess to raise or something." There's no telling how that might have impacted her life and what followed but we'll never know because she was abruptly taken out of Mrs. Long's class and placed in a tuberculosis hospital where she stayed for six months. "The only two things I remember about my stay there at the hospital," says Patsy, "is that I got my teeth fixed and I learned to sing 'La Cucaracha' because the little Mexican kids who stayed there taught it to me." She can still sing "La Cucaracha" verbatim today as if she learned it yesterday and not 70 years ago. The mind is an amazing thing. She remembers "La Cucaracha," but she doesn't remember a single day of living with her mother.

All of that upheaval and she's not even sure she ever actually had TB. She would suffer for much of her adult life from acute asthma, and perhaps her symptoms back then were an early onset of that disease. TB was nothing to be fooled with at that time and so I'm sure that those who had to make a diagnosis always erred on the side of safety for the community. So, she was whisked away, probably against her wishes.

Her stay at the TB hospital would be her last semi-stable days for quite sometime. When she was released from the hospital she went back to Orange, Texas for awhile. Then, she was sent to Liberty, Texas to live with her daddy and his Uncle Pratt. "I was nine and a half and they put me on a bus by myself to take the approximately 60 mile trip from Orange to Liberty." Hearing these stories gave me some insight into why she was so paranoid about my brothers and me traveling very far from home without her supervision. In the 60's they built one of the first shopping malls in Houston at a place called Northline. It was directly across Fulton Street and no more than 500 yards from the front door to our house. She couldn't bring herself to let us go by ourselves to that mall or to the movie theatre there no matter how long we argued with her. I never understood her protectiveness. Until I heard her tell her story.

It occurs to me now that she was only responding to the cavalier, devil-may-care attitude of her relatives who apparently thought nothing at all about putting her in harm's way, or shuffling her off to the next temporary shelter or family member. She, on the other hand, could never do that, precisely because it had been done to her. There is an old adage that says that the next generation is doomed to carry out the sins of the fathers before them. Maybe that's true. But I think that many times the next generation is completely incapable of committing the sins of their fathers and mothers. In fact, they may openly rebel against those misdeeds by digging in their heels and vowing never to treat their children the way they were treated. It certainly seems so in this case.

Huntsville

After her time in Liberty at Uncle Pratt's house she headed off to Huntsville, Texas to live with her cousins there for a short time. The hardest part of all this? "Moving around from school to school" she says. "I was the new student a lot and back then they always introduced the new student. 'Kids, I'd like you to meet our new student Patricia. Patricia is our new student.' That was difficult."

Then, she began to move around from place to place with her Grandma Bente (Mack's mother). Grandma Bente was a banty rooster, always angry, and never weighing more than 85 pounds. She woke up angry every day and got madder as the day wore on. She dipped snuff, and I'm pretty sure that didn't help her attitude any. At the end of her life she was completely blind, still always mad about something, but now not able to see you if she decided to take a swing at you.

First, they moved in with Charley and Eula. As Mom tells it, "None of these people lived stable lives." Charley and Eula argued a lot and loudly most of the time. And, they would rant and rave about Patsy and Grandma Bente as if they weren't there. Ugly stuff about how long they were going to stay and what it was costing them to keep them there, that kind of thing.

Patsy: "I was never critical of it, but I always wished I could get some place and stay put. Everybody drank a lot, and that added to the instability and craziness."

Houston

Eventually she and Grandma Bente would wind up in downtown Houston, renting one-room efficiencies in old mansions that had been refurbished specifically to rent on a weekly basis. "We lived on Lamar, and then 2100 McKinney, and then in the 1900 block of Austin, then the 900 block of Bagby across from city hall. We moved a lot because the rooms cost five dollars a week. We would move in, stay a week, be out of money, and then move to another one." These rooms were ornate, with high ceilings and fireplaces, a sink and a stove. None were painted on the inside, but they had retained some of the vestiges of their glory days, big impressive stairs and landings.

Her dad was around some during this time but not often. He and his cousin Emmett would leave for extended periods of time to "railroad" around the country. When Mack was home the house would turn into a meeting place for his drunk and disorderly friends. No one had a car back in those days, at least no one in this particular socioeconomic group, and so they would all walk over to Mac's house in the morning and start drinking immediately. Wine was 18 cents a quart back then. I'm sure it wasn't from the finest vineyards, but it got the job done for these guys. The days were spent in a stupor with a lot of arguing and discussion. Some of the more dignified ones would show up in suits and ties for these all day social gatherings. Most wore what they had on the night before when they passed out from yesterday's overindulgence.

Once, Patsy was standing behind one of these individuals when he hurled a butcher knife across the room. Apparently the Bible was the topic of discussion that particular day and, after a heated difference of opinion, one of the members of the debate team stormed back to his own room and soon returned, armed and dangerous. He threw at no one in particular, but made his point, so to speak. Thank goodness no one was in the path of the knife or it could have had horrible consequences. I'm sure Jesus was thrilled to see this tender moment in theological history.

Patsy: "I didn't think it was strange, this crazy lifestyle. I didn't really know how anybody else lived, so I thought it was normal."

When they ran out of money for booze they would take Patsy around to the Catholic Church and send her in with a note that would read something like: "Could you please let me have two or three dollars for my daughter's school supplies? I have been out of work for some time." Patsy: "The priest would give me a little money and off to the wine store we'd go. What I recall most about these events is the kindness of the priests."

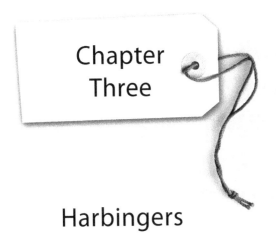

Chapter Three

Harbingers

No act of kindness, no matter how small, is ever wasted.

Aesop

During Mom's travels she would occasionally run into good-hearted people, self-described Christians who would see her plight and offer her whatever assistance they could muster in those difficult economic times. We've already noted Patricia Long, a teacher who really cared for Patsy and encouraged her. While she lived downtown, a Mrs. Borden would often come by and get her and take her out for a hamburger and malt.

She doesn't think so, but I wonder if these might have been harbingers. Like a picture of a life preserver tossed to us before we're really panicked, so that one day, when the real thing comes along and the time is right, we're sure to recognize it. For much of our lives we paddle around in the water with all of the other potential victims, keenly unaware that the ship we are all traveling on may go down, and in fact is already sinking. We choose to turn our backs to the boat so that we are able to swim worry free with all the other boat people. The water is warm and comfy. Even if the life preserver were to show up today we are not really quite sure we even need one. But, one day, events will coagulate and we will be brought to that place where we realize that sinking is no longer a remote possibility reserved for the unfortunate and weak. It could happen to us.

Many times that's when help appears. It floats in slow motion across the currents and settles down directly in front of us. Now, we have a choice to make. I wonder if everyone has signposts like this that appear throughout their lives at strategic moments and then disappear. They only last a millisecond in the overall timeline of our existence but they etch such deep impressions that even decades later, in our darkest hour, we can still recognize them for what they are. As we slowly drag our fingers across the rope and the ring we know: this is salvation. We should get out of the water, now.

As she relates the story to me, this feels like one of those moments.

Mom's memories of the good Samaritans in her young life are one of the secondary, but I think intended, consequences of true Biblical charity. The first consequence, of course, is to help a person in their genuine time of need. Period. No ulterior motive except to help. But, in doing so, there are definite impressions made, lasting ones that say that the world is not such a bad place after all. A good friend of mine, George Grant, started an organization in Humble, Texas (a suburb of Houston) called Humble Evangelicals to Limit Poverty (HELP) during the economic downturn in the Houston area in the 1980's. His church made deals with the local city fathers and elected officials, apartment owners, and small businesses. When someone in dire need approached HELP about their plight, George and his team were able to find jobs and shelter for them in exchange for work that they could do for those organizations. The people in need got help, the local folks got help, and the world probably looked very different to both after the fact.

Think about it. If you were in a desperate situation through no fault of your own, wouldn't it have a huge impact on you if someone offered assistance? Suddenly, the world takes its foot off of your neck long enough for you to stand again. The crazy world you may have been a part of fades, and another, much more friendly one appears. One that's less angry and insane. Everybody in the family is impacted in one way or another. Even if the help you offer doesn't permanently change the plight or direction of the primary receiver, the children and others on the periphery of the experience get a glimpse of kindness (maybe their first glimpse) and maybe, like Patsy, they recall it years later. There's really no telling what impact those exchanges have on the course their lives will take, or how they will view the world around them.

No Nickel, No School

Since no one had an automobile, Patsy rode buses everywhere, including to school every day. Bus rides could be had for only a nickel but she more often than not had to borrow a nickel from neighbors in her building to get to school every day. No nickel, no school. In spite of all of this, she would one day manage to get to the tenth grade before dropping out to get married. She would even be double promoted from the seventh to the ninth grade.

In all the time she was moving from one place to another, and trying to stay alive, her mother never came to see her before she left for California. Not once.

Lillian and JD

At 11, Patsy's cousin Lillian Ramsey and her husband, J.D. "came and got me" she says, "to go live in their little efficiency. Me, Lil, J.D., Aunt Gussy, Joycelyn (Lillian's sister), and Johnny (Lil and J.D.'s baby son) all lived there for awhile." It was crowded, to say the least. This decision by Lillian would be just the first of many times throughout Patsy's life that she would receive aid and advice from this couple who cared very deeply for her. Lillian and JD never made much money. He was a carpenter, and she worked various jobs, none of which paid a great deal. It didn't matter. She saw the need, she loved Mom, and she was willing to sacrifice. That was her way.

JD was a piece of work. Once you met him you would never forget him even if only for his appearance. He was an angular, dark-skinned south Louisianan. He was very tall and thin, had big bushy eyebrows, a long face, and big ears. I hear that in his younger days he was quite a golfer. He had a great sense of humor and a dry wit. He smoked, and his cigarettes were part of his "act." He would mutter witticisms under his breath while puffing away on a Winston or Kool Filter King. He appeared to not be paying attention much of the time to the endless chatter that was usually going on in the room, but, in reality, he didn't miss a thing. Later, at just the opportune moment, he would have some acidic and usually humorous commentary about something he had heard much earlier in the proceedings. His barbs and quips were priceless. He was one of my dad's favorite people. I can remember the many times they spent sitting at our bar that separated our kitchen from our living room, smoking and chatting late into the night.

Lillian was a ramrodder. She was a doer. She was saying "Just Do It" long before Nike ever thought of it. She was a very hard worker, and extremely opinionated and fiery. Argumentative is what she really was and she didn't back down from a good fight. She seemed to relish in it, in fact. She was a great defender, though, if you needed to be defended. If you were her adversary, God bless you and keep you, because you weren't going to enjoy what would happen next at all.

She was always giving JD orders, some of which he actually obeyed. I remember staying at their house in the New Orleans area after they were both old. Lil wanted JD to quit smoking and he was trying, sort of. I sat one afternoon and talked with him while he puffed away on a forbidden fag, hiding it with the deftness of Houdini when Lil entered the room, revealing it when she left, hiding it when she entered, and so on. He would tilt his head forward and look out from under his still- black and thick eyebrows, like people do when they're wearing reading glasses. "Is she coming?" he'd whisper to me. I guess that I had become the lookout, the aider and abettor of his shenanigan. I'm sure Lil had to know that he was smoking right in front of her. I'm guessing the little nicotine-laden wisps emanating from behind JD's chair gave him away. She was a lot of things, but she wasn't blind. Lillian decided not to join that battle, at least not at that time. Maybe JD was spared this time because he had company. I'm pretty sure he heard about it later.

Potatoes and Ham

Mom says she enjoyed her stay there with Lil and JD. "They liked me because I was funny. I could make them laugh by telling them jokes. I was silly."

And, there was adventure.

Once, when Lil left for three days to go to Orange, Mom and JD had an adventure. Lil had cooked a ham prior to her departure and she informed them that she had left the juice from the cooked ham in the fridge. "You guys should be able to cook your dinner with what I have left here. JD knows how to cook beans (he didn't) and you (Patsy) should know how to cook potatoes" (she didn't).

Over the next few days after school mom cooked the potatoes bit by bit, taking them off the burner, testing them, finding them to be still uncooked, and restarting them again. "After three days they had a strange glaze on them" she admits, "and they were probably not edible." While that fiasco was going on, JD was trying to cook the beans, finally giving up when he took a taste and found they were gritty, also a tad undercooked, and not terribly tasty, to say the least.

"Oh hell," he said, giving up on the charade. "Patsy, here's a couple of bucks. Just go to the burger joint down there and bring us back a couple of burgers and cokes." The potatoes wound up being eaten by the chickens that lived nearby. The beans got thrown away. "Lil never knew that or she would have killed us," laughs Patsy.

That early episode reveals something about Patsy: she has always seemed to be able to make the best of a bad situation. Her fun at The "Ramsey Mansion" came to an end when the limited space at Lil and JD's tiny apartment became even more limited when Lil's brother, Homer, came home from the service and needed a place to stay.

Mom moved back in with her Grandma Bente and started going to Jackson Junior High. It was then that she made her first really great friend, Genevieve. My mom still has an old black and white picture of Genevieve, and she was beautiful. She looked like a young Brooke Shields. She and Mom would walk to the store together for nickel cokes and soon they became inseparable. They even double dated, sort of. "No one had any money, so Genevieve and her boyfriend would come over to our place and just sit around outside." One day, they brought along a new friend, one that would become a most significant part of this story–James.

A Patsy Moment -The Rod and Reel Toss

My dad had gotten a brand new shiny rod and reel, a saltwater rig, and he couldn't wait to get out to the bay and try it out. He, Jack Jackson (Boots' husband), Boots and Mom took off bright and early one fine morning and soon, there they were, out on the water. The waves gently lapped the small boat they were riding in, the sun was shining down on them, and all seemed right with world.

When they anchored the boat and began to fish, Dad took a couple of casts with his fine new fishing gear and then, for reasons only she knows, Mom decided to borrow his new rig and give it a go. Reluctantly, he handed it over, hoping for the best. She precariously eased out onto the bow of the boat and, realizing that she did not know how to cast in the conventional way, started unreeling the line with her hand until she had a few feet available. I can imagine the conversation the fish were having with each other as they watched and waited along with everybody in the boat to see what she would do next.

Apparently she wanted to "cast" it far, so she lurched violently and… threw the whole thing into the bay. It looked like a semi-normal cast until the very last part, the part where she took both hands off the rod and flung it like the hammer throw into the depths. The four of them watched in disbelief as it hovered on top of the water for just a brief moment, and then began its long journey to the ocean floor.

Shock comes in phases. First, there was a moment of complete silence and disbelief, though I'm certain that my dad had some thoughts that could not be printed here, even if we knew what they were. Second, he probably thought about jumping in after it to try and catch it before it disappeared forever. Then, I'm guessing he had, for just a fleeting moment, the notion of throwing Mom in to retrieve it. She doesn't swim, so that would have been a little too entertaining and dangerous so he thought better of it. Finally, sadly, he came to grips with the fact that his great new saltwater rig was gone forever.

Mom says there were a couple of hours of complete silence that followed. Not a single word was spoken, until she deigned to break the silence.

"I bought that rod and reel, you know. If I wanted to, I could probably buy another one."

No response.

What ensues is living proof that God has a sense of humor and that He really does care about our insignificant stuff and He wants us to be happy. All day long they fished around trying to snag Dad's new pole, all to no avail. Mom alternated between sulking and praying for the impossible. All seemed lost as the sun began to descend. They prepared to head to shore and make the long drive back to their homes. I am pretty sure she was not looking forward to that road trip at all. She no doubt felt horrible.

Suddenly, at the last possible instant, just as Jack was firing up the boat's motor to take them home, the cork from dad's line bobbed to the top, breaking the surface of the water with unbridled joy. They rolled in the line and eventually dragged the victim back into the boat.

Yes, Dad's saltwater rig was intact, mostly. He took it home and tried to clean the salt out of it as best he could. To this day, I'm not sure if it was the salt or the emotional trauma it suffered from being pitched overboard unexpectedly, but it never completely recovered.

She bought him a new one shortly thereafter. They never spoke about it again.

Patsy & Michael, 1949

Chapter Four

Love and Marriage(s)

Is that all there is? If that's all there is, then let's keep dancing, let's break out the booze and have a ball, if that's all there is.

Peggy Lee

In a lifetime filled with surprises perhaps the biggest of all for me is that any two people ever get together and stay married. The odds of two people who are made for each other somehow meeting at a social function or work or a blind date etc.; and then hanging out and falling in love and really being able to live together has got to be astronomical. What is the old saying? You have to kiss a lot of frogs before you marry your prince? Well, only if you're lucky. Most everybody kisses a lot of frogs. Many, many people never find their prince or princess, at least not in the gushing-"I can't wait to see you and just hang out with you" sense of the word.

And, in the beginning, that was true for Patsy as well. She and James had been hanging out at her place for awhile and those dates consisted mostly of sitting around in the porch swing, talking and pitching woo.

Patsy had grown up with a somewhat modified version of the Ten Commandments preached to her on a daily basis. The version that Mack and Grandma pounded into her head on a regular basis actually only had three commandments. They were:

1) Don't steal

2) Don't tell lies

3) Don't sleep with boys until you're married

For all of her life she has abided strictly by those three commandments, and she was particularly dedicated to keeping commandment number three. She would never sleep around but in her words "I *would* run out and get married to you if you'd give me a couple of minutes to tie my hair up."

One day, while she and James were sitting around, they decided to get married. "We just sat out there and smooched a little and cooked it up," says Patsy. Not exactly fodder for any romance novels, huh? She was all of 14, and James was 17.

In truth, Patsy wanted to get away from her home and was ready to do that by just about any method she could conjure up. "My daddy had always drank," she says with some obvious sadness, "but then…his mind…he'd get mad at me and wake me up in the middle of the night and rant and rave about my mother. He just couldn't get over that. I got tired of it."

So she thought marriage was the answer, and James was handy, available and interested, so why not?

At that time, no ID was needed to get married. You just ran down to the local JP and did it. Bingo. You were hitched.

And they did just that. James told his dad that he wanted to get married. Patsy only told Pearl, a sometimes friend of hers who was old enough to sign for her. Pearl agreed to sign, advising her to "not worry about nothing, I'll tell them you're my little sister." So, off to the JP they went; Patsy, James, Pearl, and Mr. Smith (James' dad), then the next thing you know, for better or worse, they were married.

Then, they did the only thing they could afford to do: they each moved back into their respective homes and began to secretly plan for beginning their life together when they could better afford it. Patsy decided not to tell her family she was married. But her secret didn't stay a secret for long. Her cousin Emmott saw the announcement in the paper and called her father, Mack, and told him about it.

Early one morning Mack came to her and woke her up. "Patsy, when you get up I need to talk with you for a few minutes. Let's go down and get a coke."

They began to walk down the sidewalk and talk. Mack began: "Emmott came by to see me yesterday and he told me that he saw your name in the paper... that you got married."

"Yes, I did," Patsy said quietly. "Well, who did you marry?"

"I married that boy that comes down here with Genevieve and Curly."

Mack got very quiet and pensive for a minute. I hear that he was a very gentle man. I would imagine that this news hit him hard. Though he couldn't have admitted that his home was not the best place for Patsy to be, it had to be hard to hear that she was leaving, probably for good this time. I believe that most everybody deep down in their soul has paternal and maternal instincts, placed there by God, and those instincts are always alive and breathing in spite of the debris and hardships of life they often hide under. No matter what we've done or been through, the ashes of hope remain, the hope that we can pull it all together and do better. In moments like these they flicker to life and remind us that we are human.

Then, for the only time Mom can remember, Mack called Anne Laurie to discuss the situation. She was less than concerned, to say the least. She was busy with her new life in California.

And, that was it. The marriage was underway. Sixteen months later Patsy would have a son, Michael. Red-headed and small, he entered the world on December 12th, 1945. Patsy was 16. She was so young, in fact, that in some ways she and Michael have grown up together.

The marriage began disintegrating almost immediately upon its inception. A month after the nuptials they moved into one of the one- room efficiencies in the same complex that Grandma Bente and Mack lived in. It cost five dollars a week. It had two rooms- a bedroom and a kitchen. James had a job "every once in awhile" according to Patsy.

James oftentimes didn't come home at night. He ran around town with Curly, and Mom had her suspicions about what was going on. On one occasion she would find a hotel receipt in his shirt pocket. They argued a great deal. Once, when she was cross examining him about his whereabouts on the previous evening, he hit her. "He always wore two big steel rings and it left a place that I still have. That scared me, and I didn't cross him much after that."

The marriage would lurch along for another two years, but was leaking oil all the way.

Finally, in 1947 James and Patsy divorced. James married again two days after the divorce. "I was disappointed to hear that," says Patsy, "and I'm not even sure why. There was never a marriage there and certainly no love. I barely even remember him." James and his second wife, Lillian, would go on to have four children. Michael would occasionally see James and his half sisters and brothers, but, for the most part, James was uncommunicative and out of touch unless Michael instigated the call. He worked very little over the years and remained a stoic and distant individual until his death some years ago.

Mom took Michael's son Ronnie to James' funeral, "just so he would know where he came from." As she looked into the casket at him, it occurred to her that she felt like she was looking at a stranger.

Patsy & Ron with gang, circa 1950 's

Chapter Fiver

Fun and Frog #2

Love in marriage should be the accomplishment of a beautiful dream, and, not as it too often is, the end.

Alphonse Karr

After her divorce from James, Patsy bought a house on 3814 Wiley Road off of Old Humble Road in North Houston. She paid the handsome sum of $3,000 for it, 16 bucks a month. It had an outdoor toilet, but it was her house and she was glad to get it. "I always wanted a place to live," she says. I'll bet.

It was at about that time she began her illustrious car hopping career at The Corral drive in on Telephone Road, a very, very long commute, especially for someone who didn't have a car. She rode three buses every day to and from work. The Pioneer Bus would take her to Berry Road in what was then extreme north Houston. Then she would take another Pioneer bus to downtown. And finally, she would take a city bus out to Telephone Road. It would take her three hours each way, every day, at a cost of 40 cents going and 40 cents coming. In total, her commute took six hours of her day and cost her

80 cents. Her job only paid her tips (no hourly base of any kind), perhaps five bucks a day on a good day. Her dad and grandma kept Michael for her while she went off to earn the family fortune.

Any other person would have been discouraged by such circumstances, but not Patsy. "I always found a way to have a good time, no matter what was going on." She got to know all the people on her bus route and she looked forward to seeing them every day. "We laughed and cut up a lot," says Patsy and "had a great time."

One of her buddies on these joyrides was Chester Skyeagle. Chester's dad was a full-blooded Indian. Chester was a paraplegic, losing his legs at the age of 6 in a train accident. In spite of his handicap he had an infectious sense of humor. One time Patsy asked him how long he thought her bangs should be and, holding his hand down near her chin, Chester said "I'd say they should be about down to about here." Chester was a musician and played at a club in Downtown Houston. He would occasionally invite her to come by the establishment on her bus journey home and one night she decided she would take him up on it.

Frog #2
Patsy was always drawn to people who needed help. "The weaker you are, the better I like you, I guess" she says. If that is true she sure must have felt like she hit the jackpot with her second husband, Richard.

On one of her subsequent visits to Chester's club she met this tall, debonair fellow. Richard cut an impressive image, tall, with a mane of blonde hair and piercing blue eyes. Patsy was suitably impressed: "He made me think 'wow!' when he talked about himself. He said he had been in the service and graduated high school. He was the only guy I knew who had graduated high school."

As she got to know him she discovered that many of his stories were at best his overly dramatic retelling of the events in his life. At worst they were downright lies. The truth is he had been married before he met Patsy, at least once and perhaps twice. He told her that he had been married once, but the woman was crazy and ran around on him so he had to get rid of her. His sister would later tell Patsy that the story he told wasn't even close to what really happened.

He was also a thief. When he would buy a new car (usually an old clunker that he would fix up to impress) he would just steal other people's license plates so that he wouldn't have to purchase any with his own paltry funds.

While he and Patsy were dating he was arrested for license plate theft. Patsy: "He was in jail for a couple of days and when he got out he went straight to a dance hall or beer joint or something, met a girl there and married her that same night!" He was 26 or 27 at the time and this was his second marriage that she was sure about and it could have even been his third.

Somehow he finagled his way out of that marriage and set his sights on Patsy. When things began to warm up between them, Richard asked her to marry him. She then did what she would do many times in her life when she needed advice and counsel-she went out to Lil and JD's to discuss the whole thing with them. She justified her desire to marry Richard by telling them all she really knew (at least based on the shaky information he had given her) about him: He was good looking, he graduated high school and he had been in the service.

JD: "Well, what else do you know about him?" Patsy: "Well, uh, he wears a suit."

JD: "Dang it, Pattie, Dillinger wears a suit!!!!"

Despite JD's misgivings, Patsy decided once again to strictly follow the Third Commandment and rush headlong into matrimony. Lillian decided that if she was really going to go through with it, it should be a nice wedding, or at least as nice as possible. Lil made Patsy a wedding dress and her pastor conducted the ceremony. They were married in Lil and JD's house and there were even a few friends and relatives at this one. She was 17, almost 18 when she and Richard married. He was ten years her senior.

Richard didn't have a job so JD decided to put him to work with him doing carpentry. JD was a good soul and this was perhaps the greatest evidence of it. Only days before he had compared Richard to former Public Enemy # 1 John Dillinger, and here he was employing him and putting his trust in him. JD would soon find that that his trust had been severely misplaced.

Richard was a pathological liar and a kleptomaniac. One morning JD went out to his shed and all his tools were gone…missing, stolen. Even the door to the shed was gone. Lil put two and two together and figured out that Richard had to be the culprit. She called the police and they arrested him and put him in jail for two weeks. Embarrassed and stunned, Patsy separated from him, taking Michael and moving away.

But, when his case finally came up for trial, Lillian went to court to testify on his behalf!

"I believe this was a one-time thing" she told the judge. "His nature is entirely against this." Again, a tremendous act of mercy, and so like her to do something like that.

Remember this for later: She and JD never gave up on anyone. In their minds and theology, everybody was salvageable, and they really believed and acted upon that.

Richard was a smooth operator and he had Patsy completely fooled until that moment. Finally, and somewhat reluctantly, she decided to go back to him. He then decided that they should move to Kerrville because that's where his dad lived. Patsy was 21 and pregnant when they arrived in the Texas hill country. The quiet surroundings would soon be rocked by another of Richard's shenanigans.

Though it has never been proven, Richard was probably polygamous. According to Patsy he would "get up in the morning and tell me he was going to drive down and put gas in the car. That might be in January, and I wouldn't see him until July." He did that four or five times during their brief courtship and marriage.

When she was seven or eight months pregnant he pulled what turned out to be his last dirty trick on Patsy. Late one night she was at home alone with Michael and she got a loud knock on her door. It was Richard's two girl cousins. "You better get in the car Patsy and come with us. You've gotta see this. You won't believe what Richard is doing." After all she had been through I would imagine she would have believed anything. They got in the car and drove down to a local night club, and it was hopping. When they entered, there sat Richard at the head of a table filled with people Patsy had never seen before. There was a lot of laughter and they were obviously celebrating something, and Richard had his arm around a very young woman, flirting around, and putting on a show for her. When Patsy entered the club he spotted her, got directly out of his chair, hurried over to her and proceeded to twist her arm behind her back and lead her out of the place.

He was mad. "What are you doing here?" he shouted. "Go home!" Patsy had had the unmitigated gall to stumble into his engagement party. And here's a big surprise: he didn't like it.

The girl he was celebrating with was 16 and he was 30 at the time. The table was filled with her family who had obviously been taken in by his serpentine charms and couldn't have been happier or more enthusiastic about welcoming him into their family.

Patsy was crushed. Richard's cousins encouraged her to get back in there and confront him, but she didn't have the heart. She really just wanted to go home, and so they drove her back to her house. She didn't sleep well, and Richard never came home that night.

Early the next morning she awoke to another loud rap on her front door. She flung open the door to find the young girl's father and brother standing on her porch and pacing back and forth, furious and obviously out for blood.

What she didn't know was that Richard's cousins had dropped her off the night before and gone back to the club to spill the beans to the 16 year old girl's family about Richard and Patsy. They told him the truth: that Richard was already married, that the woman who they saw in the club last night was his pregnant wife, and that he couldn't marry the man's daughter even if he really ever intended to.

The girl's dad and brother had come to Patsy's house to get her side of the story. The dad began:

"Is that true? Are you really his wife?"

Patsy: "Yes. We've been married three years now."

"He told me you were just some gal he was seeing and that you were trying to lay that baby off on him, that your baby isn't his and that he didn't know whose baby you were carrying."

Patsy: "This is his baby."

"Let's see some paperwork." Though she didn't have to, Patsy produced the marriage license and showed it to them. They were beside themselves.

Patsy didn't know at the time why they were so desperate to find out the truth about Richard, but she soon learned that he had taken their daughter for a drive the night before, after the engagement party, down to Louisiana to show her some of the places where he grew up and places that were supposedly "important" to him. He was gone with the man's 16 year old daughter and the truth is they didn't really know where he had taken her or what they had been up to all night.

"That's all we need to know," said the dad. "We're calling the police." "That was it for me," says Patsy.

She stayed in Kerrville long enough to bring my brother Keith into the world on February 10, 1951. Then, shortly after that, she gathered up her things and took the bus back to Houston and moved back in with her Grandma and dad. She would finally divorce Richard in 1953.

Years before, when she was carhopping at The Corral, she had met a young man named Lee Saladino who owned a couple of drive-ins around town. She was broke, had two small children and no husband, and she needed money. So, she decided to look him up and apply for a job as a carhop at his Irvington location. Deeply discouraged, she went to work at The Winkler Drive-In #2 in 1951. She didn't know it at the time, but the love of her life would very soon pull into the Winkler parking lot in his brand new, souped-up Ford.

He was a frog too, at that moment. But in time, and with enough love, kisses, and a few miracles, he would become her prince.

A Patsy Moment - "Yonder Goes Your Momma"

Mom was frantic a lot. That caused her to develop a bad habit of leaving us places when we were young. Freud would have had a field day with this. It was a little unsettling, to say the least.

I'm sure she never meant to. She was very protective most of the time. But, there were these moments when the imp of absent mindedness would take over and then anything was in play.

One day, one fine sunny day, as I recall, Mom and my brother Keith went to Weingarten's, the local grocery store down the street a mile or so from our home. They did their bit of shopping and at that time there were porters who took your grocery cart out to a special lane next to the store, ostensibly to meet you out there and put your groceries in your car for you. That's how it's supposed to work anyway.

The first part went ok. She finished shopping, paid for her purchase, and took Keith and the groceries out to the pick-up lane. Keith waited with the porter while Mom went to get the car.

She had a lot on her mind. Other errands were waiting after this one. She was frantic.

So, instead of driving through the lane and getting her groceries, she got into her car, started it up and drove home.

"Should I get the groceries out of the car?" Michael asked. "Well, of course you should."

"Yes, ma'am."

He went outside and began to rummage through the car, looking for any sign of groceries. Nothing. He opened the trunk. No milk. No Bread. No Keith.

He came back in and told her that the car was completely empty and that something must have happened to the groceries because they weren't there, and oh, by the way his brother wasn't anywhere to be found either.

Then, as has often happened in her life, it dawned on her. Her trip to the grocery had some unfinished business! She leaped to her feet, jumped in her car, revved the engine and sped away.

When she got to the store, Keith, who I believe was quite shaken by the whole experience, was crying. I've heard that abandonment often has that impact on a person. Mom flung open the car door and, in her most casual voice (like she had intended all along to drive off and leave everything, including a relative) she said, cheerily, "Jump in, son!" He did and the porter put the groceries in the car, got his tip and ran away.

"Did you mean to leave me, Momma?" Keith asked as he got in.

"What in the world did that man say to you when he saw me get into my car and drive away?" she asked.

"He pointed at your car and said 'Yonder goes your mama…'"

Patsy

Chapter Six

"Dude"

*It's not what you take, but what you leave
behind that defines greatness.*

Edward Gardner

By 1953 Patsy was tired and disillusioned. Richard was still in her life sometimes and he would occasionally drop by for a brief visit to see Keith and then he would be off again to God knows where, disappearing for weeks and months. She finally divorced him in late 1953 and steadied herself for what appeared to be a life filled with raising Keith and Michael and taking care of her dad and grandma.

She was still a busy young woman, working a lot at The Winkler drive-in, going to Elliot Business School in downtown Houston, occasionally hanging out in the night clubs and dancing and drinking a bit. Despite the hurdles she had faced, she was still the life of the party and she always drew a crowd wherever she was. She met a lot of the famous and semi-famous people of her era, especially the well-known musicians. She became friends with Texas music legend Floyd Tillman and his band because he and some of his band members hung out at a little joint close by the Winkler. She even wrote the lyrics to a song that Tillman recorded but never released. Her song was published by Hill and Range Music Publishers.

Her drinking increased some during this time, but she was never arrested and she never missed a single day of work because of it. She definitely had the curse of alcoholic genes, though, and in time she would find the bottle too much temptation to handle especially when she was going through turmoil and strife of any kind.

The last thing she needed, really, was another troubled man in her life.

But, in he came. And he was unlike any of the men she had ever known. He was handsome in an unusual way- prematurely bald (he once told me that he could buy beer when he was 14 because he looked so much older than he actually was), with high cheekbones that gave away his strong Indian heritage and genes, very much like a young Robert Duvall. He was blue collar, a trained machinist who had done a hitch in the Navy. He had led quite a troubled youth and had many brushes with the law, mostly because of his addiction to alcohol. He was a violent young man as well, once kicking out a glass door at his house just because his dad had made him angry. Everyone in his immediate family called him "Dude" because he had enjoyed dressing up and looking natty in his youth.

That natty youth was filled with more than its share of conflict and strife. Once when he was arrested for fighting he was sitting in the back of the squad car, uncuffed. His enemy sat by the other window and between them was a large constable. While waiting, his temper got the best of him and he reached across the policeman and shoved the other boy's head through the glass window. For that brilliant move he received a shot to the eye with the cop's blackjack. "Stupid is what it was," he would say much later. "I could have lost my eye." He continued to fight a lot and was told by a psychologist when he was 18 years old that he was an incurable alcoholic. Incurable. At 18. Amazing.

Yet he had this charming and funny side as well. He was poetic and he could be kind. He didn't talk a lot but when he did it meant something. He had always had a way with girls, and the rumor was that in his youth he was especially drawn to Hispanic women. He was bright, but hadn't bothered to finish high school. He was the last person Patsy would have picked. And yet, here he was, and time would reveal that he was absolutely in the right place at the right time, for both of them.

He wheeled in to the Winkler one day in May in his brand new 1954 Ford. He had been there several times with his brother, and Patsy had caught his eye on more than one occasion. Summers in Houston are unbearable and they start in May (sometimes April) and they last until the end of September (sometimes October). These summers consist of hot, hot days, muggy nights, and high humidity, with no relief. Winkler carhops responded to this challenge by changing from their winter red outfits into their summer white uniforms. Shimmering sateen and tight is what these white uniforms were and they were apparently a big hit with Dude and the other male customers. In fact, so impressed was he that he told his brother Jimmy on one of these visits that he was going to marry Patsy someday. Jimmy passed it off as a whim, but Ron was serious. One day, he mustered up his courage to ask her out on a date, and to his surprise (and to some degree, hers) she accepted. The first date wasn't exactly something out of the movies- he took her out, bought a bag of beers (four beers, to be exact), and they sat in front of Patsy's house and drank the beers and talked.

"Before we go any further with this, I'd like to ask you to marry me" he blurted out between sips. "Marry me?" Patsy shouted back, "you don't even know me!!!!" Well, I kind of DO know you...I've been watching you for six months there at the drive in." He obviously liked what he saw. He was very persistent. Not terribly deep when it came to deciding who to marry, but persistent. Patsy said during our interviews for this book that he talked a lot about that white sateen outfit after they were married. I joked with her that he was just shallow enough to know what's important. Probably not a politically correct thing to say, but Dude wasn't pc. Not even close.

"I've got kids!" she said, hoping that might discourage him. "I don't care if you have a dozen."

He wasn't going away easily.

Enter Officer Pete

Over the next several months they continued to date. Patsy liked him and he made her laugh a lot. There were signs of trouble though, even during their brief courtship. Ron would disappear for a few days, maybe two or three weeks sometimes, and she had no idea why. During those absences other potential suitors would line up and vie for Patsy's affections. One of those gentleman callers was a Highway Patrolman, Pete. He was a dashing fellow, tall and brave, with a full head of blonde hair.

This friendship came in handy. Patsy had never driven or even owned a car at that time, and she desperately needed to get her license. Patsy's good friend Elsie ran the Winkler and was her boss. She always had Patsy's best interest at heart and decided one day to lend a helping hand. She implored Pete to help Patsy get her license. "She's gonna need a driver's license, Pete," and there ain't no way in hell she's going to be able to get one without some help." I didn't know Elsie because she died at a very young age but I do know this about her without ever even meeting her once: she was a realist.

Pete, who was interested in scoring as many points as possible with Patsy was more than happy to help her, and help her he did. She showed up early one morning at the driver's license bureau and took her written test, which she passed with flying colors. Then, Pete just happened to be the officer on duty that day (very convenient), and he climbed into her car on the passenger side to administer the driving part of the exam. It didn't start out too well.

Pete: "Okay, Patsy, push in the clutch. (Pete obviously was unaware that Patsy was having an anxiety attack and that she had completely forgotten everything that Elsie had taught her only the day before.)"

Patsy: "Which one is the clutch?"

Pete: "PLEASE LOWER YOUR LEFT FOOT!"

Pete was apparently not a patient man, and even if he was, he probably was a bit edgy, pondering the notion of driving around for a few minutes with somebody who didn't even know which pedals did what. I would guess his life flashed before him a few times during the test. He was probably thrilled to get out with everything still intact. He didn't make her parallel park (a requirement to get one's license at the time) and, sure enough, he gave her a driver's license.

Well, Pete must have thought that risking his life like that entitled him to at least a couple more dates and Patsy accommodated him. On one of these outings, they went to the Winkler together to have a drink. They were sitting in his car when Ron showed up with his brother Jimmy. He got out of his shiny Ford, walked over to the passenger window in Pete's car and asked Patsy to please step out. He looked grim. "I need to talk to you for a couple of minutes," he whispered. Patsy got out of the car and walked over to a quiet spot so they could visit.

Ron: "Who is he?"

Patsy: "He's just a friend who helped me get my driver's license. And besides, why should you care? You haven't been around in a while. I thought you had moved on."

Ron: "Well, I feel like somebody has just kicked me in the stomach!"

Patsy was flabbergasted. Here was this nice guy who she was really just casually dating (at least in her mind) and he was actually hurt by her spending time with Officer Pete. Ron had already made up his mind to marry Patsy and, in his view, her hanging out with Pete was unacceptable. Apparently Ron had ended his other relationships when he met Patsy and he was expecting her to do the same.

They continued to date after that, but sporadically, because he would come and go in and out of her life with no explanation, really.

His unexplained absences made Patsy wonder: If he hadn't been out with other women when he went away, where had he been? She would eventually learn that Ron's brand of alcoholism was particularly devastating and dangerous. He was a "binge drinker" someone who could go for months without touching a drop and then crash and burn and be out (literally and figuratively) for weeks at a time. He was young enough at the time to recover from these episodes and, in fact, recover so well that during his healthy and sober days no one would have suspected him. Patsy certainly didn't suspect anything.

But, as was his habit, he felt had to be honest with her about his problems. So, one day he told her: "I'm an alcoholic, but I'm taking medicine to help me." He was taking Anabuse, a drug that would make him violently ill when he drank. It didn't really help at all. "I didn't know what alcoholic meant at the time," says Patsy. "I thought everybody I knew was an alcoholic." The people she spoke of may have been social drinkers, but she certainly did not know anyone who had the exact problem that Ron had, or if she did, they had kept it well-hidden from her.

"He asked me to marry him every time he saw me" says Patsy. Finally, one day he made a deal with her: "I'm gonna drive by your house tomorrow morning at 10:00. If I turn the corner and I see you out there at the curb in your little red dress, I'll know you're going to marry me. If you're not there, I'll drive right on by and never come back or ask you to marry me again."

To this day, Patsy is not sure if he really meant that or not, but in any case, she was waiting the next morning out by the curb in her little red dress. Patsy recalls that it was "quite a little number, off the shoulder and slit up the side." No wonder he liked that dress so much. Apparently it and the white carhop outfit would hang in his Hall of Fame, if he had one.

He was elated that she was there. He had prefaced his drive over with a couple of beers. He was not drunk, but he was a little tight and, in her words, "happy." He and Patsy drove around and finally wound up at the Justice of the Peace in Richmond, Texas. Much to Ron's chagrin, they were closed. Patsy was getting tired and wanted to go home. But, he wasn't about to give up. They stopped and had a couple of more beers to settle their nerves and drove around until they found a little Baptist church. Ron said "Wait in the car and I'll go in and see if they're around." They were around and the pastor seemed happy to do the honors. So they went inside the church office, the faint smell of beer still lingering on their breath.

The good pastor would first need to ask them a few questions.

Pastor: "Ron, are you folks Christians?"

Ron: "Well, yes, I believe I am. My mother went to church." Pastor: "And how about you Patsy?"

Patsy had relatives who were very devout Christians but she had never spent much time with those people. She had never gotten very involved in church.

Patsy (halfheartedly): "I guess I am…"

Well apparently that was good enough for Pastor Wade O. Skinner and he joined them together in holy matrimony right there in the office of First Baptist Church, Richmond. As they left, he patted Ron on the shoulder and said "God bless you, brother Ronald." God must have been listening to Pastor Skinner, because God had just blessed him with the woman of his dreams. As the years would unfold before them these two would find that Pastor Skinner's words were prophetic: there were even more blessings in store for them, more than either of them could ever have imagined.

Patsy & Ron, 1965

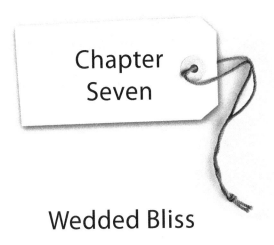

Chapter Seven

Wedded Bliss

It is true with love as it is with ghosts; everyone talks about it, but few have seen it.

Francois De La Rochefoucald

Patsy had a dilemma. At the time she married Ron she had her granny, dad, Michael and Keith living with her and she couldn't just pack up and move in with him. She would need some time and space to figure out a way to solve this problem. Ron quickly grew impatient with the idea that he was married and not only could not consummate the marriage but also couldn't even set up housekeeping with his new wife. Patsy was nonplussed and casual about it all, mainly because her feelings for him were platonic at best: "I didn't love him at the time, but I liked him." So it was definitely more important to him than to her that they come up with a better arrangement. She couldn't stay even one night away from her granny because as Patsy says, she "would call out the Marines if I wasn't at home by 11." She had a predicament on her hands and Ron wasn't helping anything by his daily queries about "spending some time together." After a few weeks Ron proposed a "honeymoon night" at some cheap motel on Airline Street. Patsy acquiesced, and things must have gone well. Soon after that encounter Patsy got much more serious about finding a place for her new husband, kids, granny and her dad. She soon found an apartment for her Grandma Bente and Mack, and a house for her, Ron and the boys.

At the end of 1954 she, Ron, Michael and Keith began their life together in a little house on Chaplin Street. Ron couldn't have been happier. He was always able to be satisfied with things as they were. Patsy, however, was already planning their next move.

She has always had an accountant's mind when it comes to financial things. She sees everything in columns of debits and credits and she has always made the little that she has suffice somehow. When in early 1955, Ron's brother Jimmy bought a house in a new subdivision on Homestead street in East Houston, Patsy decided that it would be prudent for her and Ron to buy a new house as well. She figured out how to buy a place one street over from Jimmy on Kelbourne street.

Her relationship with Ron was different than Patsy's other marriages, to say the least. Ron was honest to a fault and she never had to worry about him being a philanderer or disappearing. He worked hard and was diligent. He was probably happier than he had ever been up to that time in his life. But, alas, his malady would reappear, staying dormant for the first few months of their marriage and then, one night leaping upon him like a lion. For about two weeks he stayed mostly inebriated, passed out and asleep, waking only to drink more and sleep more. It scared Patsy. "I had never seen anything like that before. I was afraid that he would just lay down and not wake up. I was terribly worried about him." He was apparently never violent when he would have these episodes, but Patsy worried that he might accidentally hurt one of them and not even know it.

So, she began a ritual that lasted until Ron finally conquered his problem many years later. At the first sign of trouble, she would grab the kids and leave for the evening, returning only after she was sure that he had passed out. This was her way of protecting him and the kids. It was important to Patsy that his reputation with his children remain as untarnished as possible. And, indeed it did.

Ron was my dad and I only remember seeing him drunk one time in all the years I knew him. In my earliest years I remember going on those nighttime jaunts to people's homes and returning late, never having a clue at the time what it was all about. No wonder he loved her so and remained faithful to her through all the years of his life. He knew what was going on.

Real love is what it was. The kind of love that says "I'm hanging on until I can't hang on any more." Ron needed that. And, truthfully, Patsy did, too. Though she claims that she didn't really love him in those early days, she must have seen something in him that made all her efforts seem worthwhile.

A Turning Point

Patsy says that she was sassy and not terribly nice to Ron in those early years. "I told him often that I admired him, but that I didn't love him really." He was busy writing love sonnets to Patsy on an almost daily basis and she could only respond by "admiring" him.

This went on for much of the first year and finally Ron had had enough. One afternoon when he was working the second shift, he grabbed his lunchbox and went off to work, only to return a few hours later before his shift was over. He came home and put his lunch pail on the table and announced "Patsy, I have news for you, I didn't get married to be "admired." If you don't love me, fine. You don't have to live with me. But I want to stay and make this work somehow. I'm here for the duration, but not if you don't ever see yourself really loving me."

"Well," says Patsy, "that sure turned my head (and her attitude) around. I had never had a man talk to me that way and talk about staying and working at it. My heart started changing almost immediately. I decided right then and there that it wasn't fair for him to be raising my kids and not give him one of his own." She was deeply moved by his frankness, and only a few months later, told him she was ready to have his baby.

They got pregnant the very next month. Patsy says Ron was delighted with the news. He did go on a brief binge after he got the news that she was expecting, but recovered quickly and began to prepare for a new life in the household. The two of them went out and bought a book about childbirth and started reading it. Ron borrowed and slightly altered the medical term for the unborn baby and began calling me "Felix." Patsy continued to suffer from severe asthma and had to sleep upright much of the time during her pregnancy. Ron fashioned a "sleeping board" for her that just fit their bed. It allowed her to get a reasonable night's sleep and still be somewhat comfortable.

The fact that I got here at all is a miracle. Patsy's Ob-Gyn was, as she describes, "an older gentleman who had a leg injury from the war and who was taking something to deal with the pain" (probably morphine). She would later read in the Houston paper that he was arrested for drug use. He was also completely wrong about her due date. Because she went past her appointed time by almost a month, everybody was uptight, especially Ron. This was all new to him and his nerves were sometimes frayed anyway. On the night that Patsy finally went to the hospital to give birth, Ron pulled into the nurse's parking lot and, without meaning to, parked in a nurse's reserved spot. While Ron and Patsy were hurriedly getting out of the car, that nurse showed up to park in her now-taken, designated space. What ensued can only be described as a shouting match filled with expletives and name-calling. Again, God has a sense of humor, I'm sure of it. When Patsy finally went into labor, the nurse who delivered me was… that nurse. "That worked out great" says Patsy. "Exactly what you want…a nurse with a razor in her hand prepping you for childbirth, still stinging from the verbal barrage she had just gotten from your husband. Perfect."

Lil was at the hospital a lot during that time and stayed with Patsy until she actually went into labor. One of the methods used back then to get women to go into labor was walking the stairs and hallways in the hospital. For two days Lil and Patsy walked up and down the stairs over and over. Still, no baby. One day, after another fruitless trip up and down the stairs with Patsy, a breathless Lil blurted out "Patsy, I think I'm going into labor and I'm not even pregnant!"

Finally, after much hand wringing and several medically questionable maneuvers, Patsy gave birth to another son, her third. She recounts how Ron stood in the doorway of her hospital room after he had been down to the nursery to have his first look at me. Fumbling with his hat in his hand, he declared quietly but proudly to her: "It's a boy, and his head is shaped just like mine."

She can't tell that story today without choking back the tears. Apparently that's what happens when admiration turns to love.

A Patsy Moment - I see Deaf People

Mother could have an adventure almost anywhere. The most mundane circumstances would more times than not prove to be settings for the bizarre.

On this day she was in Rice Food Market, a small pre-cursor to today's giant grocery caverns. She was always rattled and in a hurry, so she devised systems to help her cope and remember things. Sometimes they worked and sometimes....well sometimes they just led to more confusion.

So that she wouldn't forget a birthday card and milk, she wrote them down on little pieces of note paper and pinned them to her blouse. When she came through the line she, for whatever reason, zoned out and entered one of her temporary catatonic states that she often visited during those crazy years of childrearing.

"That's a good idea," said the lady behind the counter, checking out Patsy's groceries and noticing her pinned-on reminder notes. Patsy stared blankly ahead.

"I say, THAT'S A GOOD IDEA YOU HAVE THERE" now adding volume to hopefully awaken Patsy from her stupor.

Still, no response from Patsy who was in fact probably enjoying this momentary respite from her hectic life.

The lady behind the counter finally gave up and finished checking the groceries, handing the receipt to Patsy when she finished.

"How much was this card?" Patsy asked, suddenly returning to the land of the living.

"OH, MY GOD!" shouted the checkout lady." "I thought you were a deaf mute."

Ron & Patsy Welch, 1958

Chapter Eight

Redemption

It's never too late to become what you might have been.

Unknown

A significant event occurred toward the end of 1953 that would impact everything in Patsy's life for the next half century. She met and re-met Boots. When they first met, Boots owned a beer joint over on Hardy Road. Patsy happened to drop by Boots' establishment on her way home from the beach and was apparently a tad underdressed for the occasion, at least according to the owner-Boots Barnes. Boots was kind enough to escort her out of the place and actually, I don't think she was very nice about it. Sometime after that Boots took the heel of her shoe and busted out an unruly customer's windshield. She didn't put up with much foolishness and she didn't back down from anybody.

That was their first meeting. Patsy never expected to see Boots again.

But then, one day an obviously distraught Boots showed up at The Winkler. She was crying and upset. Her husband had wrecked his car out in front of the drive-in only a few days earlier and Boots had decided to return to the scene of the accident, ostensibly just to get a burger and thank Elsie for taking care of her husband after the accident.

What she got instead was a friend for life. At first Patsy didn't want to wait on Boots. The memories of the episode in her bar were still fresh and stinging. Elsie told her to "get out there and wait on her. She won't bite." So, Patsy reluctantly made her way out to Boots' car, and started making casual conversation before taking her order. Patsy mentioned something about Boot's bar. "I don't own that place anymore. I've rededicated my life to Christ and I couldn't keep doing that." Like all things that Boots did, she did this religious experience in a big way. If Boots is doing it she really believes you should be doing it, too. Whatever it is. Regarding Patsy and Ronald she couldn't have been more right. They needed help and for the next 50 years Boots would be there for Patsy and her family. I'm not sure what Pat would have done without her, to be honest. Moses had Aaron, Paul had Barnabas, Stanley had Ollie. Patsy had Boots. Two peas in a pod, radically different but on a common mission, one that knit them together so tightly that nothing but death could tear them apart.

It was no accident that Boots came to the Winkler Drive-in that day, and it wasn't just happenstance that Patsy was on duty. It was meant to be.

Hiding Everything

The ensuing year or so after my birth was another rollercoaster ride for Patsy and Ron. He continued to have raging and sometimes weeks- long episodes with alcohol addiction, spiraling ever downward. More dangerous and intense with each trip down, his binges came more frequently and were increasingly devastating and lengthy. Patsy's drinking increased as well as the pressure in the household ratcheted up and up, ever higher.

Mack and Grandma Bente lived in "The Courts," a low income housing project off of Irvington Drive. Because of Ron's issues, most weekends at the Welch house were volatile and unpredictable. Patsy never knew when Ron was going to come home drunk and disorderly. So, many weekends Keith and Mike would stay at The Courts. "I didn't want them to see Ronald," says Patsy. On those weekends Keith and Michael would go to church with the Nichols family who lived near Grandma Bente and Mack. It would be Keith and Mike's first exposure to church and God and the Bible. It most certainly would not be their last.

While the older boys were spending their weekends away, Patsy would stay at the new house on Kelbourne and hope for the best. Weekdays were tougher and offered fewer options because the older boys had to go to school. "I hid everything all the time," Patsy admits. "I'd put everybody in the car and just drive." Sometimes she would drive down to the Winkler Drive-in and park under a light so that Keith and Michael could do their homework. On these jaunts, everybody got to eat hamburgers because they only cost a quarter, and in Patsy's words, "I always had a quarter."

She got to know Ron's mood swings better and soon became adept at recognizing the symptoms that preceded his increasingly frequent plummets off the wagon. He would be cold sober; then, out of the blue and at sporadic and unpredictable moments, he would get nervous and shaky; then Patsy would come home and his car would be parked crooked or even sideways in the driveway. On those days she would see his out-of-kilter car and proceed to drive on past her own house, and begin her long journey into the night. He would drink until he passed out, not always in the bed. Patsy and the boys would stay away from the house until she was relatively sure he was asleep. And then she would return, quietly tiptoeing into the house with her three sons, hoping they could be quiet enough not to wake him.

Ron would sometimes drink a half pint of vodka at a time. "I drank only for oblivion" he would later reveal in a candid testimony delivered to a room full of people in a tiny little church on Pinemont Street. On that night people who knew Ron sat in rapt attention as he delivered for the first time to friends, Sunday school students, well-wishers and loved ones his story of survival. "Nobody could tell me anything" he said in his typical brutally honest way.

He was right. Even if he had wanted to listen he could not do so much of the time because his mind was foggy from all the alcohol and abuse. During this time, Patsy tried to maintain some degree of sanity and peace in the household. Ron loved Patsy deeply and desperately wanted to keep the marriage together, but he was powerless against the dark forces that threatened to wreck their relationship and kill him.

One night, Ron had an automobile accident, running into another car from behind. He did very little damage to the other car, but it was obvious to the officer that he had been drinking and so he was hauled into the Houston jail to spend a few days. The other people in the accident sued for damages, and Patsy and Ron could not afford the lawyer's fees, so they were forced to sell their new house to make amends.

With a good deal of sadness, they moved to a rental house and began battling the lawsuit, driving back and forth to downtown

Houston and spending more time than they could have imagined with their lawyer and in court. On one of these trips it appears that they forgot to turn off the coffeepot in the house. When they returned, all they found was a smoldering pile of ashes. They recovered nothing from the debris except a stuffed dog named "Pooty." Pooty has been remarkably resilient through the years. When my wife and I were about to get married in 1980, she was given a very unusual looking package at one of the bridal showers. It turned out that Pooty was concealed inside the package. You could almost hear him breathe a sigh of relief upon his release. Ragged and haggard, he still sits in a place of honor in the Welch family household.

Trying God

As things spiraled downward, Patsy began to wonder if there would ever be any sanity in her life. One day, Lillian spoke frankly to Patsy. "It can't really get any worse can it? I know you've tried everything, Patsy, but have you tried God?"

No, in fact she hadn't tried God. The closest she came to even thinking about trying God was back there in Richmond, Texas when Pastor Skinner asked her about her relationship to Christ. After pondering Lillian's "try God" idea for a few days, Patsy decided to visit Park Temple Baptist Church. Every week she went and sat in the cavernous sanctuary and listened to the preacher talk about Jesus. She didn't understand much of what he was saying at the time, but she did notice that at the end of the sermon every week that people would come down to the front of the church and pray. Sometimes, the pastor would introduce those people to the congregation and tell them that "_____has just given their life to Christ." Patsy had no idea what that meant, but somehow it seemed attractive to her and she couldn't keep herself from coming back every week. She was "trying God" as Lillian had suggested and what she was discovering was both confusing and attractive.

Patsy couldn't stand the idea of being in front of a large crowd, and yet she somehow longed to go down front and pray. She was no theologian or Bible student so there was much she didn't know. What she was fairly sure of was that there was help there, and she had to know more about it. Every week she sat closer and closer to the front of the auditorium, promising herself that one day she would get up the nerve to walk down there and try God.

And, one day she did. From her ever-closer vantage point she walked the few steps forward that it took to get to the pastor. She knelt at the altar and confessed her sins and committed her life to Jesus. On that day, she came home from Park Temple and poured all of her alcohol down the drain. It has been almost 50 years since that day and she has never had another drink. She didn't understand all of what had happened at the time, but she knew that her life would never be the same.

Indeed it has not.

This simple act of accepting Christ has been a stumbling block for a lot of people. The idea that there is atonement for sins, that one can ask forgiveness for anything that they have done, no matter how heinous or evil, and God in his mercy forgives and forgets; that this relationship is too deep to ever understand fully is too much for some who need more. Jesus said in the New Testament that people should come to Him as a child. That means childlike simplicity, and childlike acceptance. It requires a lot of faith to just let go like that, especially if we have lived all our life pretending to know the answers or pretending not to see them even when they are standing right before our eyes.

It is precisely why some people do not even consider the option of "trying God" until they are so far down they cannot fight any longer. As Lillian said so eloquently "How much worse can it get?" That is a rhetorical question for some. The self-evident answer is that the only way to go from here is up. The "fight" in us is usually gone by the time we reach this nadir and we are overjoyed to know that we can symbolically crawl up into the Creator's arms and rest, perhaps for the first time in our embattled lives. That's what trying God means. That's what Patsy did. For that, she and all of us around here have been thankful ever since.

What Solomon Would Do

So, she got up off her knees and lived happily ever after, never facing another hardship or struggle. Right?

Not exactly.

No, they had lost their new home, and their rental house had burned to the ground. Friends, many of whom had much less in terms of earthly possessions than Patsy and Ron, gave them old furniture and mostly tattered clothing to at least tide them over until they could get back on their feet. In the interim they moved in with Ron's brother, Jimmy and their mom, Ollie Bell. Ollie Bell was a piece of work. Like Patsy, she had been married three times, with a son from each. Though she would later mellow and become my personal cheerleader and one of my favorite human beings, she was at that time rigid and stern and disliked Patsy intensely. She complained a lot about them being in her house, and when she wasn't complaining, she was criticizing. Finally after only a few days Patsy and Ron had this rather testy exchange:

Ron: "Patsy, what did you do, today?"

Patsy: "Well, I looked around some for a house for us, and I visited with some of my friends."

Ron: "Don't come back home tomorrow until you've found a place for us to live."

So, Patsy mustered up all of her courage and ventured out the next day to find a house for them to all move into.

As she struggled all day to find an affordable place, discouragement began to set in. Finally, her newfound faith caused her to do something that only a few weeks before would have been laughable: she prayed. She laid her head down on that big oversize steering wheel and asked God for help to find a home. Suddenly she heard a voice inside her head say "ask the postman, he'll know where all the vacant houses are." Hmmm...wisdom. No wonder Solomon asked for wisdom when given the opportunity to have anything he wanted. If he had been riding with Patsy that day, he might have thought of asking the postman as well. But, unfortunately he was not. So, that piece of Godly wisdom had to come from somewhere else.

And, it worked.

Patsy drove around the neighborhood and finally found the mailman and asked him about any vacancies there. Sure enough, he knew of a little place that was renting for 55 bucks a month. It was a very tiny place, not really enough room for the five of them, but she was willing to make do. As they were moving in, Boots dropped over for a visit and she was appalled. Never one to shy away from offering her opinion, she did so at the top of her lungs: "My God, Patsy! This is too small! For anybody!" Boots's mother had a much nicer house that she was trying to rent and Boots was in charge of finding a tenant for it. She started taking down the pictures Patsy was busy hanging. In her mind it was a done deal. This place wasn't going to work.

"My momma has a place, a lot nicer than this and bigger too," Boots explained in her usual shy and retiring manner. Patsy countered that "we can't afford a bigger place, Boots. We can hardly afford this place."

But Boots wouldn't take no for an answer. "How much are you paying for this?"

"55 Dollars a month."

"Then, that's gonna be the rent on momma's house. Now get to packin."

Saving Daddy

Like most people who ever met him, Boots loved Ron like a brother. She determined that she would single handedly win him to Christ if it was the last thing she did. So, during those early days after I was born Boots tried everything. She would occasionally show up with musical groups and pile out of a van that she would be driving, musical instruments in tow, all headed for our living room. These little concerts were more than Ron could handle, especially based on the condition his nerves were in. These ensembles usually had drums, a stand up bass, guitars, singers, everything.

And, they were loud. Very, very loud.

One gray afternoon Ron looked out the window and sure enough there sat a van filled to the brim with Boots and the band. He slipped out the back door and drove away just as the octet was entering the Welch house. He drove around the block for hours, circling until they at last went home.

Another time Boots showed up at the house unannounced right at dinner time. She proceeded to cry, and run her hands through her hair. Over and over again. For hours. Finally her mascara had run and her hair, in Ron's words, looked "like medusa." "Do you want that baby to turn out like you, Ron?" she asked rhetorically referring, of course, to me. He stared at her for a long time, uttering not a word. Finally he walked away. When he did return to the room she continued delivering her never-ending sermon. Suddenly, right in the middle of it she stood up, said "Oh My God! I've got to get home! I left Tommy (her husband) and the kids sitting at the dinner table while I went out to buy bread!" She had been gone for three hours.

Her fervor was admirable and the truth is there is really no way to tell what impact it had on Ron. He was very quiet. He listened a lot and he almost never showed any emotion so that you could get a hint as to the impact your words were having. My guess is he was contemplating it all and taking it all in. He was smart and he didn't forget things, especially words. He knew he was in trouble. He was certainly astute enough to know that.

On what would be one of his last trips down to the bottom, he went on a binge that lasted for weeks. Ron drank up all the family's money and every day, many times a day, he pleaded with Patsy for just one dollar.

But, she didn't have a dollar. Finally, unable to buy any legitimate store- bought liquor, he settled for rubbing alcohol. It made him very sick and soon he passed out.

Patsy was afraid he was going to die, so she called Jimmy and asked him to come by to help. "I have heard that the police will help you if you had trouble like this. They say the police will come out and lock the person up for their own good" Patsy said.

"I sure don't have any better ideas," lamented Jimmy. This was his own brother and he was going to have to call the cops to come out and arrest him. But there was nothing else they could do. Ron would die soon without some help.

So, Patsy picked up the phone and called the Houston Police and asked them to send over a squad car. Very soon an officer showed up. After hearing Ron's story, he went in, woke him up with all the sweetness and concern a father would show his son. "He was such a sweet man," Patsy recalls. "If I hadn't known better I'd believe he was an angel sent from heaven." He helped Ron get dressed, putting his socks and shoes on for him and speaking to him in hushed tones as he got him ready to take away. Ron apparently sensed that this man had his best interest at heart. He didn't put up a fight, and before long the cruiser pulled away with Ron resting in the back seat. He would spend three days in jail, sleeping and recuperating. When he got back home Boots showed up to deliver another fiery sermon, and a few days later she took him to a Pentecostal meeting where several of the parishioners spoke in tongues.

"What was all that abba-dabba-doo stuff?" he asked on the ride home. "I'm not going back there."

The Last of Richard

Right after Patsy became a Christian there occurred an episode that sounds like it came straight out of an old western movie. My dad never relayed this tale to me directly, but one of his brothers did share it with me in some detail. I'm not for violent solutions most of the time, but this one produced the desired results, so I can't really say it shouldn't have happened.

After Patsy and Ron were married, Richard would call and harass Patsy and sometimes during these exchanges he would threaten to come over and steal Keith. Patsy fended him off most of the time, but these exchanges rattled her terribly. The very idea of somebody, especially Richard, taking her children was in fact her worst nightmare. I'm sure that Ron noticed how bothered she was by these calls and, though he likely didn't talk about it very much, it probably upset him as well.

Richard had no idea who he was dealing with or else he wouldn't have risked his life and limb like that. Whatever evil pleasure he got out of it was most assuredly not worth it. Soon, on a warm Houston afternoon he would discover how foolish he had been.

Ron and his brother Jimmy worked in an oil tool manufacturing facility on Jensen Drive and after a hard day's work they would sometimes frequent the watering hole across the street from work. One night, one really bad night for Richard, Jimmy and Ron moseyed into the bar so Ron could grab a couple of cold ones before heading home and…well my uncle tells it like this:

"Your dad stood in the doorway with me for a minute and then, in a flash, he walked quickly, almost running, across the crowded room and struck up a very heated conversation with a gentleman I had never seen before. Then, he picked this man up by his shirt collar, busted a bottle on the bar and put it up to his neck, shaking and restraining himself with all he had to keep from committing murder right there on the spot."

It was Richard he was conversing with at the time and Ron was doing all the talking. While Richard quivered, his life flashing before his eyes, Ron spoke in a voice that could only be described as deeply threatening:

"You had your chance to raise those boys…now, it's my turn. Take my advice and stay away. If I hear even just a rumor that you have driven down my street or called my wife again, I'll hunt you down and find you and you won't like what happens next." He let him go

82

and Richard ran out of the bar like a Thanksgiving turkey given a chopping block reprieve. He got to keep his head, literally.

Richard was never heard from again. Not for 25 years. Not a peep. He virtually disappeared completely.

Apparently he was pretty sure that Ron meant what he said. Many years later, a very disappointed Keith would find him in San Antonio selling fish on the street corner. He was still laying low in case that crazy Indian guy was still lurking out there somewhere. He wasn't. He was long gone by then, but I would guess that the memory of that moment still lingered deep in the fish salesman's psyche.

Berry Road

Over the next four years, Patsy would take the boys and head off to Berry Road Baptist Church, a small, very conservative place of worship pastored by two former Houston Policemen. Brother Lewis, a diminutive man with a strong will, was the senior pastor. They were a rigid bunch, but Patsy found the time there valuable. She was able to learn a bit more about what had happened to her back there at Park Temple, and she learned the basics of the Bible. Every few years Berry Road Baptist Church would systematically read through and study the entire Bible. This kind of in-depth study laid a great foundation for what was to come for Patsy. There wasn't a lot of emotion at Berry Road, but she didn't need a lot of emotion- her life had been filled with plenty of that, she needed answers, and moorings.

Ron continued to drink and life got increasingly crazy. On one particularly bad night, he got drunk and took a knife and put it up to Boots' throat. "Do it!" she screamed. "Go ahead! I'm the only friend you've got left in the world." The pastors from Berry Road came over to the house and bravely took the knife away from Ron, and then prayed with Patsy and Boots. Boots was undaunted by this episode. She would remain his friend true and blue until his death in 1978. In fact, she was the only other person in his hospital room when he died.

Ron would sometimes leave the house when his binges would start. Patsy says that she worried the whole time he was sober, because she knew that any day he could fall off the wagon. Then, she worried when he was actually drinking, that he would die somewhere on the streets, or in his sleep. She was exhausted and thinking of leaving. In fact, sometimes she would threaten to leave and begin to take down the curtains and pack.

One day, after a prolonged period of sobriety, Ron came home, and on his way into the house, he bumped the door jamb by accident, a sure sign that he had begun another binge and was in fact already partially drunk and losing his balance. Patsy saw him hit the door and followed him into the bedroom where he promptly passed out, face down on their bed. She stood in the doorway, and her first thoughts were angry and vicious. But then, something remarkable happened. All those nasty feelings melted away as she stared at him, draped across the mattress, a pitiful figure who obviously couldn't help himself. Under her breath she whispered, "Well, Ronald Welch, I'm just going to love you in spite of yourself." She says that saying that was a turning point for her, a defining moment when she, hanging at the end of her rope, turned it all over to God to handle. Very soon, that decision would reap dividends.

One Sunday, not too long after this, Keith who was 6 or 7 at the time, turned around facing the back of the church from his pew near the front. "There's Daddy!!!!" he shouted with the kind of innocent joy that only kids can muster. Sure enough Ron was sitting by himself on the back row of the little church there, listening perhaps for the first time to the gospel of Jesus Christ. How His power could change a person's life and set them free from the things that bind them; and that God forgives people for what they have done, and perhaps the most beautiful thing of all for a person who just cannot forgive themselves....He forgets. Ron had always had trouble forgiving himself. Patsy says that many nights she would wake to find him sitting on the edge of the bed, smoking and contemplating. "I'm just thinking about all the stupid things I've done," he would answer when she asked what was wrong.

Patsy tried hard not to get too excited by his appearance. She so wanted to talk to him about what he had heard, but he would have none of that. He was contemplating it all, pondering what he was hearing, considering the implications and listening. He was a great listener and he was never more intent on hearing everything. Sunday after Sunday he came back again and again. He drove alone in his own car back and forth and left as soon as the service was over without socializing or meeting anyone.

One morning, after weeks of sitting on the back row and speaking to no one, he came forward and gave his life to Christ, just as Patsy had done not that many years before. He was later baptized in the cool clear waters, immersed in them- signifying the death and burial of Christ, raised again with some effort by the much smaller Brother Lewis to walk "in newness of life."

Later, in the reception line, one very wise old gentleman said these words to Ron that still ring true even today. Patsy says that there were many people who came through that line that day and they all said a lot of things, but no words more memorable or prophetic or true than these:

"Son, you have just given your children the best gift you could ever give them."

A Patsy Moment - The Wizard of Oddities

When my dad first became a Christian, he would go to church on Sunday mornings, but almost never on Sunday nights. We were Baptists, so there was always a whole night of church on Sunday nights. There was a regular service and Training Union, a kind of Sunday School except it was held on Sunday evenings. We also had Sunday school on Sunday mornings. We also went on to church on Wednesdays. If an evangelist came to our church we went EVERY NIGHT to those services as well.

We went to church a lot. I didn't get to see the second half of The Wizard of Oz until I was grown, mainly because it used to come on network TV every two years and always on a Sunday night. I would see Dorothy get whacked in the head with the window and she and Toto would start spinning and…time for Training Union.

That was just the way it was. No discussion. Just get your Bible and your good attitude and let's get going.

Well, my mom really wanted my dad to go with us on Sunday nights, but he wasn't moved to do so. He liked to watch The FBI and Bonanza and they aired on Sunday nights at 7:00 and 8:00 respectively. He really liked those shows.

Moving him to change his Sunday night routine was going to be a huge chore, but Mom felt up to the task. So, one Sunday night she decided she would start chipping away by preaching to him about the virtues and benefits of going to church rather than watching one's favorite TV shows. But, rather than preaching the sermon directly to him she preached it to me, I suppose hoping that some of the "pearls" would land on him.

"You know, Sunday is the Lord's Day" she began. "And He expects us to be in His house on His day, rather than sitting around watching TV. Then, one day, when we need help, we can call on Jesus rather than The FBI or Hoss, and He will help us in our time of need."

"Yes, ma'am," I answered, not completely sure what I was supposed to do next. She was more than happy to direct me about what would ensue.

"So, you get in that bathroom and get all scrubbed up and you and I are going to God's house. I can't speak for everybody here, but that's where you and I will be."

It was quite a sermon, lacking only a hymn and the passing of the offering plate. I went into the bathroom and took a bath, brushed my teeth, got my Bible and went outside and stood, dutifully, on the front porch while she went to the back of the driveway behind our house to back the car up.

I heard the engine start. That was good.

Then, I heard her put it in reverse. Okay, so far.

But then, as often happens with my mother, it got strange. She backed right past me and out into the road and drove away without me!!!! She didn't even cast a sideward glance my way as she backed past me in her little 65 Ford Falcon. In the time it took to walk from the front door to the back yard she had completely forgotten the sermon and the congregation of one she had delivered it to.

Scratching my head, I slowly walked back into the living room where my dad was sitting in his big chair watching TV.

"What happened?" he asked, taking his ever-present cigarette out of his mouth so he could be better understood.

"She just drove off and left me!"

"After that big sermon?" he asked, incredulous. "Yes."

"Well, kick your shoes off and watch The FBI with me."

So I did, and I watched Bonanza, too. The Wizard of Oz wasn't on that night.

Then, after I had gone to bed, Mom returned from church, stood in the doorway a minute before entering the house, and it dawned on her: "I've left Dennis at Church, Ronald, I have to go back and get him!"

She actually thought she had taken me to church. She raced out the door before Dad could tell her any different, and she was about halfway back to the church when the truth hit her.

She turned her little Falcon around and came back home.

Michael, Dennis, Patsy & Keith, circa 60's

Chapter Nine

Brothers and Bullets-Living on Deerfield Street

Nothing is so exhilarating as to be shot at with no result.

Winston Churchill

As I was preparing to write this chapter I decided to take a drive down the street I grew up on, Deerfield Street. It was a lower middle class street 40 years ago when I lived there, but now is in what can best be described as the inner city. I slowed a bit as I turned on to Bauman Road and almost immediately reached Janowski Elementary School, my school, a place laden with mostly good memories. All three of us boys attended Janowski Elementary, Burbank Junior High, and Sam Houston Senior High schools. Mom saw to that. No moving around or instability for us. Hell would freeze over before we would be uprooted. It never did and we never were. In fact, Mom and Dad bought a different house in 1974, my senior year, but that move happened only because she was assured that despite being in a different school district I would

be able to graduate with my class at Sam Houston. I pulled over to the side of the road in front of Janowski, to pause in front of what I have to admit has become a bit of a shrine for me.

I loved that place. I could read before I started school, so the principal, Mrs. McRee had taken a special interest in me, even having me tested by the University of Houston to ascertain my IQ. My parents discovered that I could read quite by surprise. Just before my fifth birthday Mom came home from Christmas shopping and said to Dad that she had been to see S-A-N-T-A C-L-A-U-S.

"Oh, Santa Claus?" I said. Well, that stopped traffic for miles around. Unbeknownst to anyone (including me) I had apparently taught myself to read phonetically. Because of those somewhat advanced skills, Mrs. McRee wanted to start me in the third grade rather than the first, but Mom opted for having me stay with my age group. That meant that we "small fries" congregated before school on a different side of the building than my brother Keith's age group. One day, he came and got me and dragged me around to his side of the building, and once he got me there, a crowd of big boys gathered around us.

"Go ahead," Keith said triumphantly, "spell it. Antidisestablishmentarianism. Go ahead. Do it!" I must have been helping him win a bet or something. I never knew one way or the other. I did feel a tad threatened, though. So, I did it:

A-N-T-I-D-I-S-E-S-T-A-B-L-I-S-H-M-E-N-T-A-R-I-A-N-I-S-M

You could have heard a pin drop. Never in the history of mankind has a group of young boys stood so silently and looked so goofy doing it. Like a gunfighter who's just proven he's the fastest and the baddest, I blew the smoke away from my mental gun and turned and strode away without saying another word. Keith swaggered, too, though he hadn't really done anything except arrange this informal gathering. He and I won a lot of respect with that one moment. I remember it like it was yesterday. The irony? None of those guys could have spelled antidisestablishmentarianism if their lives had depended on it. Not one of them. So, even if I had gotten it wrong, they would have never known the difference. As I walked away I overheard Keith brag to the group "He can spell poliomyelitis, too."

Though there was a standing rule at Janowski School that first and second graders were allowed to read books in a designated area of the library, Mrs. McRee waived it for me. I read anything I wanted, including Thirty Seconds Over Tokyo, Charlotte's Web, and The Mickey Mantle Story - all before I got out of the third grade. I loved books and I was glad Mrs. McRee had the foresight to let me read the ones I really cared about without the prescribed limitations. That was some very forward thinking at the time, I think.

The back yard of the school looked small, now some 40 years down the road. It used to seem cavernous when it was filled with relay racing, dodgeball and kickball and a half hour of unbridled activity during recess. The back fence seemed so far away when we used to run relay races against other elementary school classes. I could really run back then and I hated to lose. One time in the third grade, I was racing against a guy we called "Daddy Long Legs" who was in another class. The peer pressure was at a fever pitch when it came my time to run. We had been admonished not to take our shoes off by our teacher, Miss Mobley, who I believe I was in love with at the time. But, I could run much faster without shoes. I was on the horns of a third grade dilemma. So, I untied the strings on my shoes so that they would fly off sometime early in the contest. I was running the anchor leg and I just had to do my part. Sure enough about 10 or 15 yards away from the starting line, my shoes came off just as I planned and I wound up beating Daddy Long Legs by a length or two. I felt triumphant and proud until I looked over at Miss Mobley and saw the look on her face. She was ticked off, royally. Her eyes shot fire at me and she pointed towards the school with her long bony finger. "Go to Mrs. Eason's class and wait for me. No more PE for you today."

I would wind up going to see Mrs. McRee, but nothing really happened there. I sat around with her for a few minutes, she asked me to spell antidisestablishmentarianism, and I went back to class.

I made friends easily at Janowski School. One of those guys, Vernon, would come to my house every morning on his brand new stingray bike. He would pop a wheelie in front of my house and maintain it all the way down to the school without ever letting the front wheel touch down even once. I thought that was so cool. He could carry on a conversation and do stunts. Very impressive. I had lunch with Vernon recently. He's been through a lot of heartache in his life, but he beamed when I recounted the joy we shared in elementary school, and how impressed I was with his bike-riding prowess back then.

When John Kennedy was shot, they let school out early and I met Mom in the circle drive. That was so rare because we ALWAYS walked to and from school. Something was definitely up, though I couldn't really grasp the gravity of it at the time....odd that seeing the circle drive would remind me of that.

As I sat in front of Janowski School, I was reminded about the importance of beginnings. It shaped me in ways I cannot even describe to have some recognition for a talent that, quite frankly, I didn't give myself. I believe it came from God, but it sure meant a lot at the time to have grown people go on and on about it. They expected me to be something, and I didn't want to let them down. I'm a long way, many years now, from Janowski School and I still feel that way. "Don't be mediocre" the little voice inside me says. "Mrs. McRee is still watching…"

I resisted the urge to get out of my car and go inside. It was almost the end of the semester and I'm sure someone would have been there. Someday I will go inside and walk those halls again. And when I do, the place will be different than I remember it. That's a given. I will peer into the classrooms and I will once more think of my teachers-Mrs. Elzy, Mrs. Belk, Mrs. Rue, Mrs. Ong, Mrs. Hooks-all frozen in time at the age they were when they stood outside their rooms and greeted me as I entered. They always seemed glad to see me. That was nice. Mrs. Ong was a bit testy most of the time, but she was a rare exception among my early teachers. Mrs. Ong was my teacher in the fifth grade and by then I was a smart aleck kid who talked too much and I'm pretty sure I was cocky. Maybe she didn't appear to be happy to see me because she actually wasn't. Hmm…

I'm pretty sure that they didn't make much money for their efforts, but they all had a hand in making me the person I have become. I often wonder where those people are today. Wherever they are, I hope they have received a lot of the best this life has to offer, because they certainly deserve it. Bucking the notion that money and possessions are what it's all about they instead chose to take their college degrees and spend their days in the classroom and their nights grading papers and meeting with parents. A thankless job, really, in many ways. Some shortsighted people would call that a waste because at the end of the rainbow there is no pot of gold in the traditional sense for these folks. They probably rarely even get to see the finished product. Rather, they hand the kids off to the next grade and pick up a new batch, like an assembly line but a terribly complicated and important one. The part they add in their few months with you can be a vital one, one that you can draw on someday many years down the road when you really need it. I'll go back there...

Mustachia

I started my engine and began to head on down Bauman Road, passing Garrotsville, the street right before Deerfield. My friend Ronald Mustachia used to live (and I think still lives) on Garrotsville. I was sometimes not very nice to Ronald, mainly because he was a bit of a momma's boy and I guess I thought of him as weak. One time he kept hassling me on our walk home from school and I threatened to dunk him in the ditch filled with rainwater if he kept messing with me. Finally, I had had enough. He popped off one more time and I grabbed him by the shirt and baptized him right there on Bauman Road, right in front of the school and the school traffic patrol. When I got to Janowski School the next day I was immediately summoned down to Mrs. McRee's office and sure enough there sat an obviously reluctant Ronald and his mother. Mrs. Mustachia was a very kind person, but she could be a bit overbearing. Anyway, Mrs. McRee asked for an explanation and I told her what actually happened. She said I owed Ronald an apology and she was right. I apologized and went on back to my class. No repercussions, but that event bothers me some still today and I'm not really sure why.

I was friends with Ronald until we all got out of high school. He and I and Mark Dobrinski were like the three musketeers for years. We played every sport and Ronald's Dad was often our driver to and from The Variety Boy's Club where we would go every day of the summer and stay all day, playing basketball for hours. Both Ronald and Mark were terrific basketball players, but neither played in high school. If they had, they might have each gotten college scholarships. They were that good.

I saw Ronald again a few years ago when I was driving down Garrotsville and passed his house. His dad was standing out in front of the gate and as I drove by I slowed and rolled down my window and yelled hello to him, wondering if he would remember me. "Dennis Welch!" he cried, "Come in this house!" I pulled over and went inside and, after more than 25 years, not one thing had changed about the place. Ronald was living in a little house behind his parents' home and his little abode was filled to overflowing with books. He hadn't had a job in years and he seemed to have lost even the tiny bit of confidence he used to have. My heart went out to him. I stood in front of him and I couldn't keep from replaying the "baptismal" episode.

On this day, I probably should have turned down Garrotsville and checked on Ronald Mustachia, but I didn't. I pressed on and made the left turn onto Deerfield. Like Janowski School, I will go back one day and visit with Ronald. I think of him often, and I feel somehow that I owe him at least one more visit. I never think of him without thinking that I should have been nicer to him. I really should have.

108 Deerfield Street

Going home like this is always a little unsettling. Things are usually very different than we remember them. Deerfield seemed like such a long street back then, but now, as I turned the corner I could easily see the other end of the road and the old Northline Mall rising beyond. The houses were more run down than ever. I took my time getting there, creeping along past what used to be the Baileys', the Browns', the Kellys' and the Burktheimers'. None of those people live there now. Probably none of their descendants do either. It's not like it used to be where a piece of property stayed in the family for generations. These people who live there now have no idea about what happened in that neighborhood all those years ago. They don't know what they missed.

The first house on the left belonged to the Terry's. Kenny, Jimmy, and Dennis were about my age and were friends of mine. Their grandmother lived in a very small, mostly unpainted wood frame house. The Terry boys stayed there a lot and went to Janowski and Burbank. Sometimes they would go to the Variety Boy's Club with me, and they played the sport of the season in my yard almost every day. I never really understood their family situation but it was good that they at least had a place to go. Their grandmother was old and leathery and she walked all over the north side of Houston, picking up bottles and redeeming them at the Weingarten's Grocery Store across the street. Sometimes I would see Miss Terry ten miles or more down the road walking in a ditch or a ravine. I always felt a little sorry for those boys. They seemed destined for trouble and maybe that's what they found. Or, maybe what happened for Dad and Mom happened for them and they are somewhere living out their fulfilled lives with their wives and kids and grandkids. I sure hope so.

Past the Hall's and the Hirsch's, the Dobrinski's and the Brown's... memories began to rush in and I was transported back. The circle drive next door to the Ennis house, well, that was the scene of one of the most entertaining things that happened in our neighborhood every day. Joe McClinney delivered papers on his new Ducati motorcycle. When he would get to the circle drive he would pull through and do a 'donut', kicking up dust and little red rocks to beat the band. Sometimes he would pull a wheelie AND throw the paper simultaneously. That was very cool.

The Brown's lived across the street from the red circle drive house. Miss Brown had a son named Paul and a really nice two story house and a mean dog named 'Union'. Somebody must have gotten a really good deal on lipstick red paint. Now the whole house looks like a Monopoly hotel, only in a deeper red. Ugly. Big time.

Finally, near the end of Deerfield, it is time to see what has happened to our old two bedroom stucco house-the simply designed place that was shelter to the Welch family in the 60's and early 70's. Without any heavenly music accompanying me, I am suddenly there, sitting in front of the place, pulled over to one side of the road…

We always had the biggest yard, at least among my pals who joined me every day for our seasonal sporting events. Some enterprising person has placed another home very near our old house and in what used to be our end zone. My dad had planted two mimosa trees in our front yard and unfortunately one of them was right over our goal line. Catch a pass over the middle and get down was my advice, or else you'd run into the overhanging limbs of what was unfortunately a very healthy tree. His tree was long gone, a house planted right on top of the exact spot where it stood. Given the damage we and the rest of the neighborhood boys did to the foliage in the yard, I'm sure he would not be surprised were he to somehow hear that his beautiful mimosa had been killed by a house.

In fact, my dad tried to grow things in our yard all the time, but he soon gave up. One time, he planted this beautiful bush right on the corner of our house in the flower bed. He had a green thumb, so, of course, the bush flourished, yielding dazzling red buds and flowers in its season. One day we were all playing football and Keith sent me on a sideline pattern. "Just go ten and cut hard left. The ball will be there when you turn," he said in the huddle. So, I went ten and cut hard left and, the ball wasn't there, it was about five feet from "there" and that required me to dive directly at the house to catch it. I left my feet, launched myself parallel to the ground, stretching with all I had to reach Keith's lousy pass. It hit my fingertips on my right hand and I suddenly realized that it was catchable, but that there might be a price to pay for doing so. I flinched, but not before I had gathered the ball in securely, turned my back to the house and hit the unyielding stucco with a thud. I landed directly in the middle of Dad's beautiful bush with the lovely red flowers. The collision shook the old house a bit and before long Dad appeared on the back porch. I was a bit stunned and I continued to lie in the middle of the bush which, by the way, had significantly fewer red buds than it did only seconds before.

He never said a word to me.

He looked over the situation, shook his head ruefully and walked back in. I found out later that he went back in and told Mom that "I guess I'm not gonna be able to have anything in the yard until they're all grown. The grass won't grow because of the constant dribbling of the basketball on it. The front ditch has no grass because they take up divots hitting plastic golf balls over the house. They've worn base paths from one tree to the other (He obviously didn't understand that those three pine trees were exactly where three bases should be.), and now they're diving head first into the only healthy bush I have in the whole yard. I give up."

He ultimately did exactly what he said and gave up on having a nice yard, at least for the time being. When he and we got older and he and Mom moved to the house on Hummingbird Lane, he planted the most beautiful rose bushes and they, of course, thrived. They are still a part of that yard today, and are still as healthy as ever.

Keith

I never see the actor Steve McQueen without thinking of my brother Keith. He was a short, handsome blonde guy, very charming. He passed away in 1995 at the age of 44 from the effects of a hard life.

He wrestled for most of his adult years with manic depression and what was officially diagnosed as MS.

He always had a lot of drama going on with him, and it began at a very early age. He was all dressed up for church one Sunday morning (he was maybe 6 or 7) and mom was just finishing with getting me dressed when, in he came, covered from head to toe with rainwater and mud and what appeared to be sewage. He had been jumping back and forth across the ditch in front of our house, and apparently came up well short on one of his attempts.

"What happened to you?" Mom shouted.

"A giant crab came out of the ditch and pulled me in, Momma." Indeed. That same "giant crab" would pull him in again and again

throughout his life. He never seemed to have extended periods of peace and quiet. There were limited periods of tranquility, followed by what can only be described as intense turmoil and trouble.

Keith was a sweet guy. He would give you the shirt off his back, even if he had only one shirt to his name. He was an unusually talented person. I would call him "gifted" at certain things like crafts and carpentry. When we were very young boys we used to go to the Variety Boy's Club every day in the summer and on Saturdays during the school year. Most of the kids just played while they were there-pool, swimming, basketball, dodgeball, ping-pong, that kind of thing. But, they did have a woodshop where you could learn about woodworking and how to build things. Most kids made goofy stuff, generally unrecognizable things they proudly took home to their parents. Keith decided that he would undertake a much more ambitious project, attempting to build a gun case for our next door neighbor, Jim. For weeks he worked diligently on this huge project, finally completing it.

It turned out to be a work of art. Beautifully crafted, it all fit together perfectly and had hand carved moldings and brass handles. It was breathtaking and I couldn't believe my silly brother had built it. Keith was only about 12 at the time, and nobody really showed him how to do that. How did he learn? Genetics. Richard and his dad were both master craftsmen. When he wasn't being the world's worst husband Richard could do intricate wood work and build cabinetry to die for.

Keith became a master electrician after high school. He was one of the best in his field and fearless. He loved going up in the bucket truck and working up high. That didn't faze him a bit. In fact, it was one of his favorite things.

Women loved Keith. He would flash those blue eyes at the opposite sex and soon, he would have them in his trust. He married several times and had a son and daughter from the first two marriages. His first marriage was to a petite young blonde named Beverly, who reminded me an awful lot of Goldie Hawn. Beautiful and kind, she married Keith in a fairly large ceremony at a church here in Houston. It is important to note that one of the young men who was there that day was his best friend, Charlie. We had no idea at the time, but Charlie would come to play a central role in Patsy's family. He was someone who could be counted on, an honorable man who loved the Welch family very deeply. Ronald and Patsy cared very much for Charlie as well, and he was a regular at our house during his teens and early twenties. Like a lot of the young guys that frequented the Welch household, he had a hot car. In fact, probably the hottest of the hot. I can still see his silver Chevy II lifting its front wheels off the ground slightly as it sped away down Deerfield Street. It was bad to the bone, but its owner was good.

During their marriage, Keith, who was always something of a dare- devil, joined the National Guard as a paratrooper and went off to Louisiana to train. He didn't handle the separation very well, calling home every night, and pining away for his wife and family. He practically worshipped Ron, and being separated from him was probably as tough on Keith as being away from Beverly. The strain took its toll, and soon Keith fell very ill. The Army did all it could to figure out what the problem was, but supposedly could not pinpoint exactly what was wrong with him. He was medically discharged, but would spend much of the next two decades in and out of military hospitals undergoing tests and therapy, while slowly withering away to practically nothing. It was hard to separate his illness from the effects of his depression and a growing addiction to alcohol. They all conspired to bring him down, little by little.

Keith and Beverly would eventually have a son, Brian, a slight and winsome lad with two spindly legs that looked like they could barely hold him up. He was the apple of Ron's eye, spending a lot of time at our house just hanging out and being adored. In fact, when Dad had less than a week to live, he sent for Brian and the little fellow came over and stayed by his side and brought him what was probably his last bit of joy here on this earth.

Keith's marriage to Beverly became very strained and would eventually end in divorce. His behavior became more and more erratic as the years passed.

He would remarry, once again to a great person who loved him dearly, a young lady named Cheryl. They had a daughter, Mandy, who has grown up to look very much like Keith. She has beautiful piercing blue eyes filled with kindness, a very pretty girl. When you look in her face it is hard not to see him. He'd be very proud.

Keith hardly ever saw his kids after the divorces, and I believe that caused him a great deal of pain. Charlie would, several years after the divorce, fall in love with and marry Beverly and would raise Brian along with two other boys they would bear together, Shannon and Brandon. Charlie was a terrific father. Keith could not have asked for better homes for Brian or Mandy to be raised in. Cheryl remarried as well, to a terrific individual named Buddy. He raised Mandy as his own, providing stability, guidance and love for her. In some ways, these homes were very much like the house Keith was raised in. I was Ron's only blood son, but you would never know that by the way we were all treated. He raised us the same way, disciplined us the same, praised us the same, took the same joy in our successes, and treated the grandchildren the same. I didn't have any children when Dad died, but I can't imagine that he would have loved them any more than he loved Michael's or Keith's kids. And, that's the way it should be. These men made the decision to raise these children as their own and never looked back.

A recent event in my own life helped me better understand this power of commitment. My son married a young lady who had a 5 year old daughter, Alexis. She only recently joined our family and yet she is already the center of all things in the Welch household. She is one of us. How did that happen? I think it's supernatural. We decided as a family to commit our lives to her and "adopt" her, and from that moment on, she was family. Period. We don't introduce her as "our step granddaughter" or "our little adopted granddaughter." Nope. She's a Welch. It's my first experience like this and I find it to be fascinating. The secret, I think, is the depth of commitment. A half hearted determination to adopt her into the family doesn't produce the same experience. A father or mother who only gives lip service to being mom or dad to someone else's children, never gets the full adoption experience. It is my understanding that Bob Hope adopted several children. He was often asked which ones were adopted and which ones were his blood children. He would answer "I can't remember." Great answer, and one that I now understand fully. Kids raised by parents and grandparents who are willing to make that kind of commitment are blessed indeed. Brian and Mandy were blessed kids, and they know it.

And, speaking of grandchildren, Alexis now has a little brother, Matthew. He is 3 as I write this and he too has moved to the center of our lives along with Alexis. I carry pictures in my billfold of them both, but I resolved not to be one of "those" grandfathers who pull out the scroll of pictures and show them to complete strangers. I guess I thought it was much more dignified to wait till people actually ask to see the grandkids. Well, I recently threw my "dignity" out the window on a plane that was stuck on the tarmac in Chicago's Midway Airport. We sat for the longest time, then before I knew it I was showing all the strangers around me those beautiful little faces. And you know what? It felt great! We're a lot less dignified around here and we're having a ball going to the park, learning to swing, riding the rides, and hanging out together with no real goal in mind except to hang out together. All that undignified stuff does our hearts good and grows us together as a family.

Dignity is over-rated, as it turns out.

Brian's Wedding

After Brian was grown he called me one day and asked me to go play golf with him, that he had something he needed to talk with me about. While we were out on the links he let me know that he was going to marry a great girl that he had been dating for a long time, a young lady named Connie. He wondered if he should invite Keith to the wedding. Keith was living in Louisiana at the time, just outside of New Orleans in a little town called Metairie. I told him that it I thought it would be a nice gesture to send an invitation to Keith. "He probably won't come, Brian, but he'll be sure to frame the invitation. It will mean a lot to him."

Sure enough, Brian sent Keith an invitation, and much to our surprise, he called to tell us that he was going to fly over for the wedding and stay just for the night and go home. He was quite ill by this time and almost completely disabled. Michael and Mom picked him up at the airport and began the 30 minute drive up to the church in New Caney where the wedding would take place. He had to stop by the roadside several times on the way because riding in the car made him violently ill. When he got to the church he stayed in the car until after the service had started, mainly because he was embarrassed about his appearance, and probably about his life in general. After the service was over, Brian went out to Keith and spent a long time talking to him, a conversation that has never been shared with anyone that I know of.

I sang in the wedding and then sat near the back, leaving room in the very crowded church for the family and friends of the bride and groom. Keith sat next to me, quietly taking it all in. Mandy was one of the bridesmaids. He hadn't seen her in many years, basically since she was a small child. As the bridesmaids made their way down the aisle, he leaned over to me and asked a question that still makes me sad, even just to write it down, let alone hear: "Which one is Mandy?" He had paid a heavy price for his decisions. This should have been his life, his day, and in his heart, he knew that. "That's her, Keith," I said pointing her out as she passed by us. His eyes never left her as she made her way to the altar. His heart was obviously broken, and this would be all he could handle. He left as soon as the service was over and went back to Louisiana.

A few months after the wedding, Brian and Mandy decided to take the seven hour drive over to Metairie and spend the weekend with Keith. Brian walked in first, surprising him. Mandy waited around the corner, then, sprang into the room. It was almost too much for him. They had a glorious weekend together. The stay was even extended a bit because a bad storm blew through South Louisiana, forcing them to wait an extra day before returning to Houston.

Not long after that I got the call that nobody wants to get. It was Keith, ringing me midday at work, asking me if I had a few minutes to talk with him, that it was very important. Through the years I had gotten a lot of calls from Keith, sometimes in the middle of the night. I had become jaded a bit to his "important" calls. This one seemed different, though. For one thing he was stone sober. In fact, the past two years had been better for him in many ways, and he had stayed clean and sober for most of that time. He lived near Lil and JD, and went to a little church near his house. He even played guitar in the church band, and made a few friends. He could always make friends.

He began the conversation: "I think I'm dying, Dennis." Wow. He had escaped death at least a hundred times and never even mentioned it. Here he was, candidly admitting that it was near. "I think I can go in peace, now." The rest of his conversation told me why. He talked at length about the visit from Brian and Mandy, laughing a little about their prank and about how surprised he was that they even thought of doing such a thing. It obviously meant the world to him, to know that there was no bad blood between them, no hard feelings, that they cared enough to come all the way down to his little house in Louisiana to see him. It was huge. He beamed about that moment, and I could feel his pride through the phone. That was unfinished business, and their visit finished it in a way he could not only deal with, but die with.

"I think I'll probably last a couple of weeks at most. I just wanted to say goodbye." He also wanted to tell me a secret he had been hiding for more than 20 years. It explained a lot, though I wasn't really sure if I believed it at the time. "I don't have MS, Dennis, and I never have. The doctors just called it that because they couldn't say what was really wrong with me without giving away what I really did while I was in the military. I was sent to Southeast Asia on a secret mission and I was bitten by a mosquito that was indigenous to SE Asia. Somehow, I got a disease like encephalitis, and my body never recovered."

During the years after he got out of the military he would often tell people that he was in "Nam." Michael, who served 14 months there, would be furious when Keith would make that claim. They argued every time they were together and Keith would say that. Keith lived in San Antonio for awhile, a city filled with military personnel and war veterans. He would occasionally march in the "Silver Wings' Parade," organized by Viet Nam vets. That really riled Michael: "They're going to kill you sometime, Keith, when they find out that the closest you ever came to Nam was buying your cigarettes from a Vietnamese man at a convenience store in Louisiana." He would swear that he had been there, but it seemed impossible. He was only in the military for less than a year, much of that time spent in and out of hospitals.

He concluded our final conversation with this: "I just wanted you to know the truth." We said our goodbyes, and somehow it felt very final. No drama this time, no wild eyed tales of adventure. It was all very quiet and reserved, as if everything in his life had been settled, and it was time to see what's next. I am still thankful today that he called me. Many people do not get the chance to say their goodbyes. That was important to both of us.

A couple of weeks after that, Patsy got a call from the Veteran's hospital in Metairie, asking her to please come down, that things looked very grim for Keith. She immediately hopped on a Southwest Airlines jet and went down to be by his side. During that first night she called me at home, crying. "They're asking me to give the okay to remove him from life support, and I don't think I can do that. I have until tomorrow morning to make the decision." She was distraught, and rightfully so. Keith had driven her crazy through the years, but nothing is stronger than a mother's love. We prayed on the phone for God to intervene somehow. She went back to Lil and JD's to spend the night, and before morning, the angels came and got Keith and took him to heaven. I am very thankful that she didn't have to make that difficult and painful decision.

He was buried in the Veteran's cemetery in Houston. A few friends and family attended, and then they all came back to Patsy's for a little coffee and cake and to tell "Keith stories." Everybody had one. Years ago, we were all watching the evening news and they were telling the story about a man who accidentally drove his back loader into a mud pit and was drowning. A bystander who obviously wasn't afraid for his life tied a rope on himself and jumped in and rescued him. Standing behind the reporter was that man: Keith. He was like Forrest Gump. He always seemed to be in the middle of chaos and seemed to be able to keep his head about him even when no one else seemed to be able to.

Another time he was driving in San Antonio with our Uncle Sonny. It was a very rainy and nasty night, and, according to Sonny, they had each had had "a sip or two." All of a sudden, Keith let out a blood curdling scream at the top of his lungs: "STOP!!!!" Sonny slammed on his brakes, Keith swung the door open and started running full speed across an open field. He had somehow seen in his peripheral vision two cars collide. He arrived before the paramedics and saved two lives, dragging them from their cars and administering CPR. When the EMT's showed up they greeted him by name. "Hey Keith, thanks for your help, man." Uncle Sonny was stunned. Everybody knew Keith.

But, he saved his best story for last. When Patsy and Susie went in to purchase Keith's plot and headstone, the lady at the cemetery said "Would you like to have us put Viet Nam veteran on his marker?"

"Why would we want that?" queried Patsy, "He didn't go overseas."

"Yes, he did," she affirmed emphatically. She produced his DD-214, the official document of his service to his country. And there it was in black and white.

I miss him.

Michael

Every month from a distant sky it came-a reel to reel tape wrapped in plain brown paper and bearing the name of PFC Michael J. Simmons, Viet Nam. He was my brother, and it was at once unsettling and comforting to hear his voice. My mother usually cried a little when he would begin to speak.

"Hello, this is Michael," the tape would begin, as if we didn't know who would be sending a tape all the way from Viet Nam. Michael was always kind of formal like that, and he has always marched to the beat of his own drummer. In high school, he shunned the cool cars and clothes of his day and rode a bicycle all over town. He worked at the "Dairy

Dream" over on Irvington Drive, and that trip was many miles from our house. He never missed a day as I recall, a testament to his ability to stick with the plan, even if it was his own plan, and even if it included difficulties and challenges most people would avoid.

His boss at the Dairy Dream called him "Creeping Jesus" because he moved sort of slow, and because he spent all of his break time reading his Bible. He is smart. He taught himself to read Greek and Hebrew while he was still in high school. He has staying power. When he undertakes a task he doesn't quit until it's done. He graduated from college and majored in Greek and Hebrew. When he was a very young kid, he was so skinny you could see his bones sticking out. He decided that he would take up weightlifting. For years he lifted weights and drank all the protein drinks and before we knew it he was a chiseled specimen.

He also became, as Eddie Murphy says, a "Karate Man." He was determined to learn karate and Judo, and in typical Michael fashion, he bought some books and learned how to break a brick and how to remove your heart with his bare hand while it was still thumping (we never saw him do that, actually, but Keith and I were convinced he could do it, so we didn't have a lot of cross words with him). He could break a house brick in half with his bare hand. It was fun to bring my friends around to watch him do that. I probably could have sold tickets.

One time, his karate expertise came in real handy. We had these wooden barstools that were pretty worn out and Mom wasn't going to get rid of them until they literally fell down. That was her way. They were still usable, so why spend the money? That is why she still has enough money. No whims, no impulse buys. Anyway, these barstools creaked and sometimes leaned a little when people sat in them. That alone was not enough to convince Mom of their potential dangers. Dad, on the other hand, was less than thrilled with them. When a good friend of the family, Edith (who happened to be pregnant at the time) sat one night, creaking and leaning, Dad had seen enough. The next day he ordered Michael to take the barstools out behind the garage and in his words "make kindling out of them." All afternoon I heard Michael out behind the garage, giving the official karate yell over and over again interrupted only by the sound of snapping wood. He made kindling out of those barstools, all right. There was hardly a piece left that was longer than six inches. You give Mike a task, he does it. The Army must have loved that quality in him.

His faith made him fearless. When other young men were heading for Canada to avoid the draft, Michael never considered that, and dutifully went to the Army to serve his country. I remember the day he left for Viet Nam, and my dad's prayer at our dinner table the night before, and how his voice broke when he asked God to watch over my brother as he faced the perils of war. His voice broke. More evidence of Dad's commitment to Michael. People who don't commit don't care like that. They don't care deeply if they are not fully invested in the outcome. Michael didn't carry Dad's last name, but he was a full member of his family nonetheless. Dad never cried much, at least not in public. But, he had a deep soul, and moments like this gave a little insight into what really mattered to him. It was hard not to cry with him.

It was also hard not to worry about Michael. The numbers on the daily news were not encouraging. Thousands were dying; and the Houston Chronicle would report every day that a transport helicopter had gone down or that an American base camp had been napalmed. Much of this happened near Michael. He was in the thick of it, and we prayed every morning before school for his safety.

Then, those tapes would show up. Michael's voice would be strong and courageous. After introducing himself again, he would say "I'd like to sing a song for you now." We would all gather around the kitchen table to listen, the hum of the old reel to reel tape machine ever present. Michael always had his guitar and his Bible with him, and my guess is he wore out both of them on this tour of duty. He began to sing:

"O Lord My God, when I in awesome wonder..." and the sound of gunfire and the zing of ricocheting bullets could be heard in the distance, but his voice never wavered and he didn't miss a note.

"Consider all the worlds thy hands have made..." low flying planes, strafing the jungle and destroying a piece of one of those worlds, thundered overhead, overdriving the tape, slightly distorting the hymn.

"Then sings my soul, my Savior, God, to thee..." no dry eyes at the table now. The curious mixture of a familiar voice surrounded by weapons bent on silencing it was too much to bear for some of us. Michael sang on, though, and every month for all 14 months he was there, he kept on singing.

Then, one day he came home. He has never talked much about Viet Nam, but a friend of his who served with him there told us that Michael would volunteer for the most dangerous duty because he believed that he had an angel who watched over him, and that everybody has an appointed time to die. He reasoned that he was completely safe if it wasn't his time. He was greatly admired for his actions. In fact, "Creeping Jesus" was something of a hero and considered to be one of the bravest in his platoon.

He married Debbie and had four terrific kids: Timmy, Ronnie, Randy, and Faith. All four of them have the most tender of hearts, and their kindness is infectious. I can honestly say that I have never met sweeter people. They are all grown now, and in fact Tim and Ron are serving in the U.S. Military and have been to Iraq on extended missions. When those boys speak about their experience they use some of the same language Mike used to describe his time there in Viet Nam. They, too, are unafraid. Michael has instilled his simple faith in their hearts and they are reaping the benefits of knowing that there's only so much they can do, and the rest is up to God. So far, they haven't sent me any CD's of "How Great Thou Art," but I wouldn't be surprised at all if they did.

Michael is still an unusual guy who hears a different rhythm in his life. He is married now to a wonderful gal named Rosie, and they have a very comfortable life together. One recent event let me know that the old adage about not being able to change people is really true. I moved to Georgia in 2001 and before I left I encouraged him to get a pager or a cell phone so that Mom wouldn't have to drive to his house to find him. "You've got to be more communicative, Mike," I admonished.

A couple of weeks passed and then I got a call: "Dennis, uh, this is Mike." (He is still introducing himself.) "In an effort to be more communicative, I have purchased a pager."

It was a miracle. But then…

"And this is how it's going to work."

I reminded him that I had not one but two college degrees and that I knew how pagers work. "I call you. Then, I put in my number and you call me back, right?"

Michael: "Well, no. You are number three."

Number three? I was crushed. I didn't even understand the new pager system he had devised yet and already my feelings were hurt.

"Number three??? How can I be Number three Michael? I'm your brother. Who the heck are one and two???"

He calmly continued: "Rosie (his current wife) is one, and Mom is two." Well, I felt a bit better. I started calming down a little.

"Okay, I'm good with that."

He seemed glad to hear it. He went on with his instructions: "Okay. You'll call me, type in the number three, and I'll call you back."

I said, "Well Michael, I have a potential hurdle for you. What happens if I'm not at the number three? How are you going to know where to call me? Most phone numbers have at least ten digits with the area code and everything."

He was undaunted and unbowed. "We'll burn that bridge when we come to it. Let's just try it."

So, a couple of days passed and I did exactly what he told me to do. I have to admit that I felt a tad foolish typing in just the number three and the pound sign, but I'm not one to make trouble, so I did it, and I began to wait for his call back.

And waited. And waited.

He called me TWO DAYS LATER!!!! "Michael!!!! What if I was bleeding or something horrible? TWO DAYS??? I can walk to your house in a day and a half!"

He was very repentant about the two day time lapse, so we decided to try it again, to give it one more chance. So, I waited a few days and then I dialed the pager, dutifully put in the number three, and in only a few hours the phone rang.

"Hello. This is Rosie. You rang?"

I was stunned. "What are you doing calling me Rosie? I paged Michael."

"He gave me the pager. It was too much trouble for him."

One phone call in a week was too much trouble for Michael. That speaks volumes about him. He is good hearted and generous. He is pretty gentle and sometimes even a bit outgoing. But, he enjoys his solitude and his time with Rosie. He doesn't need much. He's not needy. He is content with what he has, and if, on that rare occasion, he thinks that something he doesn't have would make his life better he gets it. I was with him recently right after he had bought the latest and coolest Dell laptop computer. True to form, we went into the local bookstore and he bought a giant book about Windows XP, and I'll bet that even now he is perfecting his keystroke and studying every detail of that computer, how it works and what all it can do.

Patsy, 1967

Chapter Ten

Healing

A bodily disease which we look upon as a whole and entire within itself, may, after all, be but a symptom of some ailment in the spiritual part.

Nathaniel Hawthorne

---

108 Deerfield was a tiny place, really. It had two bedrooms, one bath, a fair sized living area, a very small kitchen, an attic fan, and a stand alone wooden garage in the back. The driveway was long and the yard was surrounded by a chain link fence. There were enough trees in the yard, but for the most part, it was very open. I have no problem remembering every nook and cranny of that house. I can go back there in my mind anytime I want and remember it all. In some ways it's easier to think about it as it was, rather than go by and see it as it actually is.

We lived there through the tumultuous 60's. By this time Mom and Dad were attending Thornton Street Baptist Church on a regular basis and had made some good friends that would prove to be lifelong companions. Dad was not attending Sunday school but would drive Mom over to the church at the appropriate time so she could attend. Then, he would go the five or so miles back home and get dressed and return for the regular church service at 10:45. As he became a more familiar face at the church, he would often be stopped by well-meaning parishioners who would ask him to stay for Sunday school. "I can't," he'd say. "Patsy won't let me in the bathroom in the morning and we just have the one bathroom." That was his way of saying I'm thinking about it but I'll do it when I think the time is right. Eventually he overcame those pesky bathroom logistics and started coming to Sunday school, and before long, he was asked to teach a men's class. He was a wonderful teacher. Very smart, and everybody liked him. He just was who he was. No pretense. That played very well at this particular religious establishment. It played pretty well everywhere in his life, actually.

Mom was taken with the kindness she was shown at Thornton Street and immediately loved the place and the people. Most of the aspects of her life were getting better but she still had some fairly major physical issues to deal with. She had wrestled through most of her life with acute asthma, often spending days and days sleeping in a chair and gasping for breath. Though she had always had problems with the disease it began a rapid deterioration so that by the summer of 1967 she really thought she was on her deathbed. She was not quite 38 years old at the time.

She lost 30 pounds off of her already rail thin frame. Our family doctor, Doctor McClimans, tried everything to help her, all to no avail. Finally and reluctantly, he urged her to get an oxygen tent and prepare for life as an invalid.

Over the years she had tried everything, all kinds of oddball cures including one that involved buying a Chihuahua dog. Patsy: "I really don't know what I was thinking. I guess I was desperate…the dog didn't help a bit and in fact, developed some breathing problems himself." At least she can laugh about it now.

Years before, she had a doctor who prescribed adrenaline for her asthma attacks, even teaching her how to administer shots to herself so that she could deal with the problem immediately. "That could have killed me," she says. True. At that time she was living in a garage apartment behind Lil and JD and they helped her build a makeshift oxygen tent. "That could have killed me, too," she says. Why we didn't blow the whole house up with that contraption is beyond me."

On this day in the summer of '67 she was growing weary of the constant battle and she felt she couldn't go on. She called Michael in and said "Son, if you come in here some day and I'm gone… you know where I'm going. Don't be afraid." But, Michael *was* afraid. He was 21 at the time and he was a Bible student in a big way, teaching himself to read Greek and Hebrew so that he could better understand the nuances of the Holy text. Michael's understanding of the Scriptures gave him an idea. If God could heal people in the Bible, why can't he still do that? Could it be that it doesn't happen because we don't ask for it?

Mom's Cousin Homer also believed in divine healing and Michael knew that, so one day, when Homer was there, he decided that they should pray together for Patsy's healing. He woke Mom up. "Mom, wake up. Homer is here. We're gonna pray for you."

Homer knelt on one side of the chair, Michael knelt on the other and they each held Mom's hand and began to pray out loud, asking God to do a miracle. "By the time they were done praying," says Patsy, "I started feeling a bit better. By nightfall, I was able to function some and move around. By the next morning all evidence of asthma was gone completely." She's nearly 80 now, and she has never had asthma again, nor taken any medications to prevent its return.

I also had severe asthma until I was 12 or so. One Sunday morning I was so weak that I couldn't sit up in church at all. I was with my grandmother and we were attending her church, Evangelistic Temple on 11th Street in Houston. It was a big church and a very charismatic place with a lot of sort of Pentecostal trappings, speaking in tongues and so forth. Thankfully, they believed in divine healing, too. Every Sunday, parishioners would fill out an orange card to ask the Pastor, Pastor Wilkerson, to pray for them during the Sunday morning service. On this day my grandmother sent my name up on the orange card. Pastor Wilkerson began: "Mrs. Garraway's grandson is with us today and he has asthma. Mrs. Garraway has asked us to pray for him this morning and to ask God to heal him." I don't remember anything at all about the prayer itself, but I do distinctly remember this: By the time the service was over I could go back to my grandma's house and play basketball. I've never had asthma again, either. That was 1968.

JUL 62

MY FIRST SUNDAY SCHOOL CLASS '62

Patsy's First Sunday School Class, 1962

Chapter Eleven

Missions of Mercy

Teach me to feel another's woe. To hide the fault I see; that the mercy I show to others; that mercy also show to me.

Alexander Pope

Bobbie

There was always a lot of activity at our house on Deerfield Street. There were people coming and going at all hours, cars parked in the driveway and out front in the street, phones ringing off the wall. I'm sure that some of our neighbors thought, "Yep, those Welches are running guns or gambling or something there at that house." No, we weren't dealing in drugs or guns there. We were dealing with people's hearts and lives. Growing up in that home taught me that a lot of people lead lives of not so quiet desperation. Divorces, sickness, heartache and pain- all of it came through our doors and sat at our bar and told it to "the bartender." In this case the setup was a cup of coffee, the milk of human kindness, the water and bread of life. People found answers there, and they kept coming back and bringing their friends and relatives.

One of these was a very diminutive gal named Bobbie. She lived next door with her husband Chuck, and her son. One morning Mom drove past their house and saw Chuck out in the front yard setting fire to Bobbie's clothes. He was drunk and out of his head, and after they were fully ablaze he must have had a twinge of guilt and began furiously stamping them out, to no avail. He burned her clothes up. Anger and alcoholism combined, a bad combination for everybody.

Shortly after that, Bobbie showed up on our doorstep with her 5 year- old son, pounding loudly on our door in obvious alarm and desperation. When Mom opened the door, Bobbie asked if they could come inside and hide. She was wearing only a half-slip with a towel wrapped around her torso. They stayed with us for a couple of nights, hiding out from Chuck who was on a drunken rampage. I walked past their house on my way to school and saw Chuck passed out on the doorstep. He didn't even make it into the house the night before. He would do what alcoholics do…wake up from this stupor long enough to get behind the wheel, drive to the local liquor store or bar and start the process all over again. He was very dangerous. He always had a gun on him and, in fact, the morning that Bobbie showed up on our porch, she told us that he was going to shoot her if he could find her. In fact, earlier that morning he had put a bullet in the ceiling and that had rightfully driven her out the door and over to our house for refuge.

On the first night of their sojourn at the Welch house, an event that still chills me took place. Bobbie's son and I were sitting in my room talking, and all of a sudden he reached into his mother's purse, pulled out a loaded 25 caliber automatic pistol and pointed it straight at my face.

"I could shoot you if I wanted to," he said. We were little kids, and he didn't know that he could have killed me. But he certainly could have. One slip, and he probably would have finished me right there. Guardian angels? You can believe whatever you want.

Soon after that, Bobbie and her son went down to Boots' house to stay. She had a back bedroom and a bit more space than us, so she took them in, with no clue as to how long they were going to stay. Boots always had people coming and going in her house. It was like a hotel. Her husband, Jack, was growing tired of people being there. She snuck Bobbie and her son in to a back bedroom. Boots warned them: "Now, don't come out. The bathroom is right there, and I'll bring you food." Boots also had some of her grandkids staying with her. She had made them a bunch of corn dogs. When the kids wanted more corn dogs, Boots said "no, you can't have these last corn dogs. They're for a lady and a little boy who are staying in the back bedroom." Like kids often do, they went to Jack and asked him if they could have the last corn dogs, hoping he would be more willing. When Jack said yes, one of the little girls said, "Well, Deedaw (the name the grandkids all called her) said that we can't have them because they are for a lady and a little boy who are staying in the back bedroom." Jack went to Boots and said "Why did you tell those kids that damn lie? They think there's a lady and some kid in that bedroom over there." Boots began, "Well, Jack"…and promptly fessed up. Jack was a good man, and generous, too. He just needed to account for all his corn dogs.

Another time, Bobbie made a run for it, but hid out in another house, not Patsy's or Boots'. Thinking she was at Boots' house, Chuck showed up on her doorstep and demanded to see Bobbie, his ever present gun bulging in his pants pocket and occasionally glistening in the afternoon sun. Boots told him to hang on and she locked the door and went and called the man who was the interim pastor of the church. "What should I do?" Boots asked. "Well, Miss Boots, you should probably just shoot his kneecaps out. I wouldn't kill him, though. But that should take care of him until the authorities arrive." He was kidding, of course, but somehow his prescription seemed appropriate given the times.

After awhile, Boots and Mom did with Bobbie what they did with everybody they hung out with, they invited her to church. She attended for several weeks and listened carefully to the sermons. It was all new information for her, but she kept coming back for more. Eventually she did what Patsy and Boots had done-she went down to the front of the church, prayed for forgiveness, and made a commitment to Christ. She was baptized soon after that, and her life changed in many ways. They eventually moved back to Alabama but not before one more episode that involved guns and booze. Chuck showed up at Thornton Street Baptist Church one night demanding to know where Bobbie was. She was actually in the church service, which was well underway at the time. Chuck was drinking again, and, as usual, he had a gun in his pocket. Frank Cooper, one of the mildest and kindest people you would ever want to meet, somehow got picked to go out to meet Chuck in the foyer of the church, not knowing what he might do. He calmed him, and nothing violent happened.

Bobbie and Chuck would eventually divorce. No surprise there. What is remarkable is that years later, when Chuck was near death, Bobbie took him in and cared for him until he died. It was obvious from that experience that Bobbie had learned something from the life of Jesus. It's easy to wear little bracelets that say What Would Jesus Do? It's another thing entirely to actually do what you think Jesus would do, especially when every family member and every fiber of your being wants you to take revenge and be angry and give people back in kind what they've given to you. Bobbie is a feisty character, and I would guess, not prone to give up easily or to forget Chuck's transgressions. But, she did it anyway. Forgiveness is a powerful decision, and it is just that-a decision that we make to let go and move on. Bobbie had been forgiven and she knew it. It was time to mete out some of that same kind of forgiveness, and Chuck, a pitiful soul who was too far gone to fix himself, happened to be the beneficiary. From what I understand, that's exactly what Jesus would do.

Over the past 35 years Patsy and Bobbie have stayed in touch, mostly by telephone and letters. Patsy has done extensive Bible studies with Bobbie, all or mostly all over the long distance wires. Bobbie says that there is a "spiritual link" between her and Mom. Perhaps. Just a very few years ago, Patsy was the victim of a thief who took one of her checks and wrote it for $70. She found out the next morning when she went to get some money out of her checking account. When she got back home that morning, she went out to her mailbox and there was a letter from Bobbie with a check for $35 inside. She called Bobbie to thank her, and during that conversation, Bobbie asked out of the blue. "Patsy. Does the figure $70 mean anything to you?"

"Well, yes," said Patsy. "That's the exact amount that somebody took from me."

"I thought so," said Bobbie, lowering her voice a bit as she pondered the situation. "While I was praying a few nights ago, the Lord told me to send you $70 dollars, but I didn't think I could afford that amount, so I sent $35. The other $35 will be in the mail today. Don't give it another thought."

Bobbie has prospered over the years and that episode has happened once again. When Patsy's house was flooded and virtually destroyed in 2001, Bobbie sent a substantial amount of money to help pay for the restoration, and furniture. Patsy never asked for it, nor mentioned her need. Bobbie just heard God tell her how much to send and when to send it.

And Bobbie obeyed. She would be the first to tell you her life is better for it.

Ginny

It was a typical Houston summer day when Patsy stopped into the convenience store just down from her house to buy a cold coke. When she was getting her money out of her purse, she did what she often did when she felt led to speak to someone about her faith-she pulled a gospel tract from her bag and handed it to the lady behind the counter.

"I probably don't need this," the lady said, motioning toward the back door of the establishment, "but that gal out behind the store could sure use it." Patsy walked slowly over to the back door and saw a woman, bleeding and slumped against the wall. The lady behind the counter walked over to Patsy and handed her a towel. "She'll probably need this, too." Patsy walked slowly over to the sad figure and, without saying a word, began to wipe the blood off of her face. "She lives in that trailer over there" said the counter lady, "go tell her family to come get her," Patsy went over to the trailer and knocked on the door and let them know that this woman, who turned out be named Ginny, was over at the store, and that she was in very bad shape. They didn't seem surprised to hear the news, and promised that they would go right over and bring her home.

Patsy left and went on home. For most people that would be the end of the story, a good deed done, an act of kindness above and beyond the call of duty. After all, she had only stopped to buy a cold drink. Her actions were more than most people would have done under the same circumstances. Like Cain, we would ask "Are we our brother's keeper?"

Of course we are, but acknowledging that fact forces us to pay attention, to not ignore those we find suffering, especially when we can do something about it. Patsy believed that. She was learning about Jesus every week in church, and one of the things she knew is that He never ignored the plight of those around him, and He never half-healed anyone. If he touched them they were completely whole.

So, the next day Patsy returned to the little trailer house that Ginny lived in with her husband and her mother and dad. She sat with Ginny and her family and learned more about this stranger she had discovered behind the store. She was married to a radio personality, had struggled with alcoholism for years, was only in her mid 30's (though she looked much older), was bright and articulate, and very, very ill. Much of her hair had fallen out, and her skin looked old and yellow and diseased. Patsy asked her if she'd like to come to church with her and Ronald. Over the next few months she attended Thornton Street Baptist Church, sitting in the very back of the sanctuary in her wheel chair, listening with all she had to the story of redemption and forgiveness.

One day, without any provocation, she just stopped drinking altogether. Her mind began to clear up, and she asked if she could be baptized. Ginny could walk a little but only from the car to the church, and then she had to return to her wheelchair. Ronald and Milton Black wouldn't let that stop her from being baptized. They carried her in her wheelchair, down into the baptistry, and baptized her one Sunday evening in the name of the Father, The Son, and The Holy Ghost.

Over the next few months Ginny remained sober, but her health, already in serious decline from the years of abuse, continued to spiral downward. She began to hemorrhage internally and was placed in the Medical Arts Building in Houston for observation and treatment. After several weeks the doctors finally got the bleeding under control. Ginny was moved to a rehab center where she was told that she would never walk again. She cried when she told Patsy the bad news. "The doctors say I will never walk again...but I WILL walk again."

Ginny was in rehab for the next two years. Her thick dark brown hair grew back and her skin cleared up and became beautiful and clear. Patsy and Boots saw her as often as possible and prayed with her and for her as she went through this ordeal.

After she got out of rehab, Patsy went and got her and brought her back to our house so that Ron could see her transformation. Without telling him who she was, Patsy walked into the room with Ginny at her side. "Do you know who this is?" she asked Ron. "No, I don't believe I do." He didn't even recognize her. "This is Ginny!" exclaimed Patsy. Another miracle in what would be a lifetime of miracles in Patsy's life.

Ginny lived four more years, mostly healthy and happy. Though her life had been cut short by years of abuse and struggle she got the opportunity at the end to taste for a brief moment the good life, the life of health and joy and peace that is a part of what the Christian life offers. The world knows more than they probably need to know about the negative aspects of not knowing God. The Church has done a pretty good job of communicating that. Unfortunately most people know very little about the blessings of God, the health and longevity promised for a life well-lived. The real Christian life of the Bible turns out to be a very sane life, one where you love your neighbor as yourself, where you are your brother's keeper, where being a trustworthy and honest person actually adds years to your life. The book of Proverbs says you even sleep better if you choose this path. The Bible is filled with that information as well as story after story to illustrate it in every imaginable way. And yet, I think most people are painfully unaware. So, they press on as best they can, traveling without The Map, hoping to arrive with as few scars as possible.

The Danger of Anger

For most of the past 35 years Patsy has taught at least one weekly Bible study in a home or a Sunday School class or both. These classes typically begin with the offering of prayer requests for anyone who is in need themselves or knows someone who is. Many years ago, a young lady asked for prayer for her dad, an otherwise intelligent and sane man who had been locked up in a mental ward at the Veteran's Hospital in Houston for sometime. He had lived a good life, a quiet existence with his wife and family. Then, one day, quite unexpectedly, his wife left him for another man.

He almost immediately went mad. His anger and resentment welled up inside of him and would not let him rest. Finally, his family had him committed.

"Pray for my daddy," his daughter, Carolyn, said. She gave a simple overview of his condition, and every week, for several months, the group mentioned his name in their prayer time, asking God to help him through this crisis somehow.

Then, one day, Patsy got a call from the lady. She said, "You won't believe this, but they let my father out today and he's here with me in my house. Would you come by and see him sometime?"

Patsy and her good friend Robbie Jordan drove across town, knocked on her door, and went inside, not knowing really what to expect. Would he be dangerous? Was he still angry? Medicated? Catatonic? Instead, what they found was, as Patsy describes it, a "handsome man, with sharp features, grey at the temples and distinguished looking." He sat quiet and resolute. When he opened his mouth, he revealed that he had no teeth. They had been ground completely down during his stay in the institution, mainly because his intense anger had caused him to grind them even in his sleep.

Patsy and Robbie sat down in front of him, but he looked straight ahead as if they weren't there at all. Patsy began: "Sir, Carolyn has been very concerned about you and we've been praying for you every week."

Silence.

They tried again and again to speak with him, but he ignored them and stared straight ahead. Finally, they got up to go. "We're going to go, now," Patsy began, "is there anything specific that we can pray about with you before we go?"

After a brief silence…"Yes, my back is in terrible shape," he said, stunning them a bit with this sudden outpouring of oratory.

Patsy collected herself a bit and responded: "Sir, I know you've had a lot of struggles in life…I don't want to discuss all of that painful stuff right now. But, the Bible says that if we are going to pray for healing, we also have to ask for forgiveness of sin. Is there anything in your life you're holding against God or anybody in this world?"

Suddenly his demeanor changed. He turned beet red and began beating violently on the arms of his chair and screaming at the top of his lungs "I hate them! I hate them! I hate them!" over and over again until he broke down in tears and wept uncontrollably.

Patsy was unshaken by this episode, and once he got reasonably quiet, she calmly continued. "We are going to pray to God for you and with you. Are you willing to forgive them?"

Slowly he raised his head until he faced the two of them head on, this broken man who had lived for so long with anger and insanity. "I know there's no other way. I forgive them." They prayed and not only did his back improve, but his whole life improved. His sister invited him to her church, bought him some new clothes, and paid for his dental work. Though he did not live terribly long after this, he returned to some sense of normalcy and his mind was clear until the day he died.

A Patsy Moment - Delivering the Avon

The 60's were a great time at the Welch family compound. Patsy and Ronald began to have some semblance of a normal life and a stable household. Dad always had a "hot" car that he was driving or working on. Mom went to cosmetology school and sold Avon. She was one of the top producers at Avon and had many great friends and customers. She liked all the rah-rah meetings and she made enough extra money to keep the family's financial ship afloat.

One time, the two (hot cars and Avon) intersected and the results were (as they often were with Mom) strange and funny. Mom's car had some problems so she had to take Dad's Ford Galaxy out to deliver the Avon that week. His car had a 427 cubic inch engine in it and it was so very fast. He called it "Old Bruiser." It had a four-speed shifter on the floor and it loped along like a dragster. It wasn't particularly loud, but it was mean and could burn the tires without even trying. The clutch was a heavy duty racing clutch that Mom could hardly press down, even when she used both feet.

Not exactly what you'd expect to see your Avon lady driving. But the Avon (like the mail) had to be delivered. So, off she went, loping along, rumbling down the little streets in her territory. I'm guessing that at that very moment Patsy could stake her claim to being the fastest Avon Lady in history. She was riding the wild stallion and there was no thought of turning back, even when it became apparent that she couldn't get the car to stop in front of the correct house so she could make her delivery. The clutch was stiff and uncooperative and so gearing down and slowing was an issue. Customers looked out their windows and saw their sweet Avon lady driving back and forth past their homes, trying to rein in the mighty steed she was using as a delivery vehicle. Finally after a few tries she succeeded.

Once the Avon was safely delivered, she would set off to begin the same process all over again- loping, braking, sweat- ing, slowing, stopping, and delivering. Her response to this escapade revealed a lot about why she won sales awards at Avon, and on a bigger scale why she survived all the bad moments in her life and changed her little piece of the world for the better. She came home laughing about it. Yes, all the Avon got delivered, and she even had fun doing it.

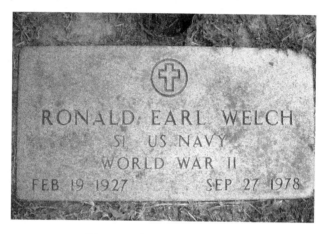

Picture of dad's headstone

Chapter Twelve

The Lion Sleeps

Death never takes the wise man by surprise.
He is always ready to go.

Jean De La Fontaine

There is probably nothing in this world that affects a young person like the loss of their father. This is especially true if that father has been a good man, a good role model, a mentor, and a hero. I had just turned

22 when we got the news that Dad was sick. I chose not to accept that news at all. Instead, I chose to assume that the best was going to happen, that healing and a long life was in the cards for him. But, alas, it was not to be. Looking back, I wish I had prepared better for what was to come.

On that February afternoon in 1978 I did what I always did: my well-rehearsed daily routine. I went to classes at The University of Houston and I came home before going to my part time job at

Sleep-N-Aire Mattress Company. I still lived at home at the time, the only perk my parents could provide for me while I attended college at The University of Houston. I was in my junior year and well on my way to getting a business degree. I paid for school and they let me live at home and eat their food for free. On this day as I entered the house through the back door Mom looked a bit grim and sort of ashen, and she was sitting at our bar that separated the kitchen from the living area. She seemed tired and her words came out like it was all she could do to make them leave her body and creep across the airwaves to me. She said, in almost a whisper, "Maybe you should sit down for a few minutes before you go." She looked down, pausing to collect herself. "I think you should know that for some time your dad has been feeling something like a clenched fist in his left lung. He went into the doctor to have it tested and it turns out that it's cancer."

Cancer. I see that word on the page today and I get it. At the time I didn't understand it at all.

She said it without emotion, really-like she was reporting the news. Maybe we were both afraid to respond negatively by crying or calling it bad news. Maybe we thought that not acknowledging the gravity of the announcement would somehow prod God into jumping right in and fixing it. Whatever the reason, I remember the tone as being serious but not somber. God could certainly choose to heal him. But...would He?

Ronald Welch was invincible, a mighty man who had overcome all his obstacles and lived to tell about it. He was strong. His muscles rippled when he turned a wrench, his tanned arms filling up the sleeve of his pocket t-shirt...cigarettes always available in the pocket. He had not an ounce of fat on him anywhere. No marshmallow middle for this guy. All man, all the time.

People loved him. He was becoming more and more comfortable in his own skin, more outgoing in his 40's, often staying at church gatherings long past his usual bedtime. My mom had even taken to driving her own car to church parties because she knew that Dad would be staying until the wee hours.

He was wise. The years of turmoil and trouble had taken their toll in some ways, but they had made him one of the wisest and wittiest in all the land. The truth about life was etched on his heart like chiseled granite. He certainly knew what trouble looked like and how to avoid it. People came to him for advice all the time, especially young people. He loved young people and had a particular concern for young men who were just starting out in life trying to raise a family and do right. For a long time he and Mom had a Sunday night Bible study in our house on Deerfield for the young fellas in our church and their wives and girlfriends. These guys would show up with their Bibles in hand and a copy of Hot Rod magazine in their hip pockets. After the lesson was through, the discussion would inevitably turn to fast cars and big powerful engines. Those kids would all go down to the beach in Galveston on Sunday morning and show up that evening at our doorstep still pouring sand out of their shoes. They may have missed Sunday School, but they never missed Church at the Welch's. They were always there.

When he spoke to this group they would sit in rapt attention. They knew. Ronald Welch was no pretender. He had been *there*, wherever there was. He spoke with intensity but without any shouting and histrionics. His look could pierce you and his message could as well. Keep your nose clean, love your wife, don't be addicted to anything but the Truth, and don't let anyone or anything rule your life except for Jesus Christ. Life can be grand if you don't try to outsmart God. That was his message. Simple and digestible.

He loved the Book of Proverbs. Supposedly written mostly by King Solomon, it contains a blueprint for avoiding trouble and strife. It tells you how you can live a long life and prosper. It also tells you how easy it is to fall in with the wrong people and be led astray. It tells you that when you *are* led astray you might not make it out alive. So, be careful. He liked Solomon's admonitions, as well he should. He had lived both sides of Proverbs, barely getting out with his skin and sanity intact. He still carried some of the outward scars of his troubled youth, but his forgiven heart was clean and unharmed. Some he had known and hung out with were not so lucky. He hoped that his lessons would be heeded by this living room filled with young lives with bright futures. Redemption does that to a person. It makes you care in a way that is indescribable. Once you've been rescued it colors your world completely. You have to tell someone. You have to warn them of the consequences of missteps and transgression. You have to. If you care…you just have to.

Dad was an enigma in some ways. For one thing, he hardly ever played ball with us in the yard, but occasionally he would step out on the back porch and without any warm-up at all he would throw a couple of uncatchable knuckleballs to one of us. A knuckleball is a very difficult pitch to master. If you've never seen one, I'll try to describe it. It leaves the pitcher's hand at about half the speed of his fastball and a good one doesn't spin at all. It hops along in a completely unpredictable fashion and is so very difficult to catch. In fact, catchers usually wear bigger mitts when they have a knuckleballer on the mound in hopes of catching the ball or at least knocking it down. He eventually taught me how to throw it and I used it often to get the boys in pony league to strike out. My question? How did he master the knuckleball? Who taught him that? I thought his troubled youth was filled with only troubling things, not playing pitch and being coached to throw like that. I never asked him.

He loved deeply but he didn't always talk about it. In fact he almost never talked about it. But, there were those moments when you just knew. I can still feel him standing next to me in the foyer of our church and he would reach across with his strong hands and grip my shoulder. A little thing, but very reassuring. It said "I'm probably not going to say it out loud, but I care very deeply for you and I'm here for you." It meant more than words, believe me. When these days I am running around like a chicken with my head cut off and trying to make big decisions for myself and my family, I could really use one of those reassuring squeezes.

Spiraling Down

The seven months from that dark day in February until September 27th are really a blur, in retrospect. We put dad's name on the prayer chain so that his church friends and family could pray for him. He began to take radiation treatments out at the Medical Center in Houston, one of the world's best at treating the disease. The tumor was on the upper part of his left lung. The doctors said there was no doubt about it: smoking was the culprit and the tumor was fast moving and deadly. He began almost immediately to look tired and a tad gaunt as the treatments and the disease began to sap the life out of him. He temporarily stopped working, taking a leave of absence with the full intention of going back when he recovered. The little bit of hair he had started falling out and the slow march to death's door began in earnest.

Within a few weeks the tumor metastasized and spread to his brain and other parts of his body. We prayed harder and I continued to dis- believe what I was seeing. I just couldn't accept it and I wouldn't. He stopped driving for the most part and loaned me his almost-new

Chevy truck to use until I could get another car. He told me that he hoped to re-claim his truck someday. At least that's what he said when he handed me the keys. I wonder today if he ever intended to take it back. He was probably looking out for me, letting me down easy, though I wasn't giving up or conceding anything.

Just a few weeks before his death he did a very unusual thing that says a lot about the man and how far he had come in his life and what his priorities were. He decided to take what would be his last drive over to an old Houston neighborhood where his Uncle Abe lived. Uncle Abe was old and had lived a pretty good life but had never been much of a churchgoer or a follower of Christ. Dad somehow managed to find his way to the neighborhood, but upon his arrival he found he couldn't remember exactly which house Abe lived in. He got out of his truck and stood looking around at every house, hoping that something would spark his memory. He was weak and tired and this was quickly turning into an ordeal. Just as he was giving up, Abe miraculously appeared outside his door and saw Dad standing beside the road. He came across to get him, greeting him. "Dude, (Abe, and all the other Welch's, still called him by his nickname given in his childhood), good to see ya. Come in this house." Dad had driven all the way across town to tell Abe one last time about Jesus and what a difference He had made in his life, and how that Heaven awaits those who accept Him as their savior.

Just a couple of years after Dad died, I got a call from my grandmother (Abe's sister). She wanted me to come to North Central Baptist Church to see Abe get baptized. Whatever Dad said must have had an impact. The truth is, the change in Dad's life was more powerful than his words could ever be. Abe would later say that he had been watching "Dude" all those years to see if what he had was the real deal. By the time Dad made his difficult journey across town, the verdict was already in. Whatever had happened to him back

144

there at Berry Road Baptist Church had changed him forever, and Abe knew in his heart that it had to be supernatural. He had known Dad in his darkest and most violent hours. He had seen "Dude" for awhile at his worst, and he had seen him for a very long time at his best. It was enough to convince him to follow.

Last Days

One day in late summer, Dad and I were sitting out on the front porch enjoying the afternoon. By this time he was a mere image of his former self. He looked much older than his 51 years, his eyes were hollow and he was very thin. He still came to church most Sundays, but he needed a wheelchair to get in and out of the place. It was very hard to watch, but I found myself spending more and more time with him rather than less. My mind told me that he was really dying but my heart wouldn't let me believe it. I wanted to pull away and not watch what was happening to him and yet I couldn't waste a second of the precious time he had left. So, we hung out on the porch and visited and waxed more philosophical than ever. I had somehow become able to buy another car so I offered him his Chevy truck back. "No," he said quietly and thoughtfully. "You keep it. I'll let you know when I want it back." More signals about how this was going to end. Hard to hear, and even harder to come to grips with.

He was a smart guy...

So smart in fact that a few years before he had stopped being a machinist and gone to work at an ARCO refinery in Pasadena, Texas, and began to learn all he could about the complicated refining "Unit" he worked on. It was the best job he ever had, the most money he ever made, and probably the most recognition he ever got for a job well done. Both his brothers were hired before him and they convinced him to apply. It was such a great gig for him for a lot of little reasons. For example, he worked a rotating shift and he liked working "doubles" (two consecutive eight hour shifts) because the cafeteria would bring him a menu and he could order anything he wanted for whatever meal he was missing. He would often have steak and potatoes with green beans. It was all part of the deal. He was getting a taste of the good life from a company that really liked and appreciated him. He was well-liked and he liked the people he worked with a great deal. To his credit he mellowed a bit and became more accepting of certain things and people. A lot of the guys he worked with wore longer hair and beards (he would have called them hippies before), and there were many blacks and Hispanics and he befriended them all.

One event let me know that his transformation was complete. He came home from work one afternoon with a "single" of Willie Nelson's "Blue Eyes Crying in the Rain." There was Willie on the cover with a big shock of red hair and a full beard and bandana. He was a sight. When I was a young boy, there used to be country and western shows that ran every Saturday night from about 6:00 to 10:00. One of those shows was the Ernest Tubb Show. Willie was a weekly guest and usually performed one song on the show. He was already a successful songwriter (he wrote "Hello Walls" and "Crazy," two huge hits of the era) but he was at that time a struggling recording artist without a record deal. He was clean shaven and wore a very typical C&W outfit with a string tie. EVERY WEEK my dad would say "Son, go turn down the sound until that guy is done." Every week. He hated watching Willie sing so much that every week he couldn't bear to hear even one note.

And here he was, years later, bringing home one of Willie's recordings. Dad only bought two records in all the years I knew him. This was a big moment, and I hated to spoil it for him...but just I had to tell him. "Dad, do you know who that is?"

"Why, sure I do son. This is Willie Nelson. Why do you ask? "

"Well, Dad, this is the same guy you had me turn the sound down on all those years ago. Every single week we did that! Did you know that?"

We both laughed out loud at the situation. You know, he didn't have an answer. What's most telling, though, is that even though Willie looked like a "Hippie," Dad looked past that and bought his record anyway because the song was good. That little event seems like a small thing to the outside world, but it says a lot about how much he had grown during the past few years. He learned something about ignorance. It's bliss until you're exposed to the truth. He had a choice. He could have done what a lot of people do and denied the truth.

Or, he could embrace it. That Willie record told me that he was choosing the latter. I was proud of him.

Eventually he was asked to become a foreman on his unit. The test for that job would require that he learn the chemistry and science of how his unit worked. It was very complicated stuff and not for the ignorant or faint of heart. He took that on with a vengeance, staying up late at night and poring over the manual page by page. He took the test and passed with flying colors. He would later turn the job down when it was officially offered because he was sure that there was someone more qualified who would come along. I call that the "Welch man syndrome." It's the notion that I am not good enough and that there has to be someone else out there who is. Though he had convinced himself that he was forgiven, he never convinced himself of his real worth. He never knew his value in this world to other people. Maybe he knows now.

Tending the Garden

Dad had a garden, a little ten by ten space behind the garage that he tended and looked after with great care and love. That thing was like some kind of atomic garden, producing enough vegetables to feed a small country. The only other garden I would ever compare it to was my grandmother's, Ron's mom, Ollie Bell. She could do that, too. Her garden was bigger because she had more land to deal with. Hers produced more food than she could ever eat, so she wound up giving away peas and beets and tomatoes every year. Maybe green thumbs are hereditary.

Anyway, when Dad's health allowed, he was out there weeding and picking and doing who knows what. Whatever he did worked magnificently. The vegetables were perfect and sweet. He loved that thing almost as much as he loved his cars, and his roses that he planted along the front fence line.

One day, I stepped out in the yard and saw an image that has remained etched-clear as glass-in my memory. Dad was sitting on the ground outside of the garden, and his brother, my Uncle Jimmy, was inside the garden on his hands and knees picking weeds and doing all the things Dad could no longer do. The idea was that Jimmy would make sure Dad's garden didn't suffer from neglect, and one day, when he was better, he would reclaim his rightful place there. Every week he came by at some point, put on his gloves and sat in the dirt, talking with Dad, picking the ripe vegetables, hanging out. No fanfare, no trumpets sounding, no look-at-me spotlights.

It was a very simple act of brotherly love and servanthood. Surely Jimmy had other things to do. And yet, here he was, picking weeds out of his brother's garden. It's one thing to talk about love and putting others first, it's another thing entirely to actually do it. When it happens it has a profound impact on even the casual observer.

I will never forget that act of kindness. I don't see my Uncle Jimmy that often anymore, but when I do I always take the time to remind him about that good deed, and thank him.

Saying Goodbye

On the morning of September 16th I walked into Dad's bedroom to say goodbye as I did every day. He had fallen the night before and in his panic he had reached for the towel rack in his bathroom. It tore from the wall and he fell, unable to get himself up to get back into his bed. He was embarrassed about that. He was still the old lion in his own mind and heart. Lions don't stumble.

I believe that the "Old Lion" theory explains why older men have a tendency to pick up the check at restaurants, especially when they are with their children or grandchildren. That simple act of paying says "I can still chew the leather if I want to." Old men want to prove that they can still hang, and be productive and useful. Clint Eastwood proves it by making Academy award winning films at 75. But everybody's not Clint Eastwood. Each man has his own way of bowing his back and facing the uncertain future, one where strength inevitably wanes and can be counted on less and less. The "Old Lion" theory. Trust me. It works.

Well, my goodbye this morning was different. He was not well and he was painfully cognizant of that fact. He probably ached from his fall and he was tired of fighting this battle.

"How you feeling?" I asked. "Not good."

"I mean, how are you feeling…about all of this?"

It was then that he delivered his "25 year reprieve" comments. "Somebody should have killed me years ago…" And he went on about what a great life he had been given and how he had had a chance to have a great wife and family. I didn't know it until later, but he was telling me goodbye and my unwillingness to believe that he was actually going anywhere caused me to miss the significance of this important preamble to his final exit from this world and from our lives.

I was still in denial.

"Well, goodbye Dad. I'll see you this afternoon when I get home from school."

We would never speak again.

"He was always ahead of us"

I would dare say that Earthman Funeral Home had rarely seen anything exactly like it. The place was jammed with people standing around every wall, the back of the auditorium completely packed. I don't believe the place could have held one more person. Brother James, Dad's pastor, gave the sermon that day, and lauded him as if he had been a President or CEO. He was only 51 when he died and I think every person in that room thought that was way too young for Ronald Welch to be taken from this world.

Who would have thought it? This fairly non-descript guy who never ran a country or a company, never was on TV or radio, never accomplished any of the so called "big" things; and here he was with so many people who loved him that we couldn't get them all in the place. What a change. I contend that if he had died at 30, hardly anyone would have attended or cared. Somehow, those last 20 or so years of sanity and relative serenity produced this. Once again, he had a chance to taste how life is supposed to be, and he had a significant impact on so many during those two decades that, at the end, he is held in such a place of esteem and honor. It was a miracle, really. There is a verse in the Bible about how the end of a man's days should be better than his beginning, if he trusted and obeyed God. That was certainly true for Ron.

I can hardly remember anything about that day. It was all a blur, a feeling of disbelief that this was really happening. I was mad at God. Wasn't He listening? This is not what I asked for at all!

The only thing I remember with crystal clarity is this: after the eulogy was delivered people were allowed to pass by the casket and take one last look at him. Then, they would file by the family and offer their condolences. I'm sure everybody had good things to say, but after almost 30 years I can only remember one comment, seared into my psyche, apparently to dwell there forever. Pauline Johnston, surely one of the most gracious and thoughtful people to ever walk this earth, stepped up to the family and said "Patsy, I am somehow not surprised that the Lord took him before any of us. He was always ahead of us, wasn't he?"

Yes, he was.

A Ron Moment - Driver's Education

Dad always had a certain look about him when he was about to go out on Hardy Road and "blow his car out," as he called it. He usually wore an old straw hat (I'm not sure what that symbolized) and his ever- present blue jeans and pocket tee shirt. One summer, he was taking me to my driver's ed class and he had on the uniform, straw hat and all.

"You going to go blow your car out?" I asked, already knowing the answer.

"Nope. I'm going by the hardware store and pick up some nails and fix the garage."

Hmmm. I didn't believe him, but I didn't pursue it any further. He dropped me off at the front door of Sam Houston High and drove away, the tail pipes roaring as he turned onto Irvington Road. He definitely wasn't headed toward the hardware store.

My driver's ed car had three drivers: me, a big tall kid named Rick, and a little fellow named Garland. I felt kind of sorry for Garland. He was so short that he had to lean up to look through the steering wheel to drive. On this day, he was the first driver. We all buckled ourselves in- Mr. Denson, our instructor, in the front passenger's seat, Rick and I in the back, and Garland at the wheel.

We started off very slowly and turned on to Hardy Road. It made me a little nervous when Garland drove because it seemed like we weaved a lot and the wheel was too big for him to handle. We lumbered along very slowly in our green '73 Cutlass, Mr. Denson continuously encouraging Garland and advising him on what was going to happen next.

What actually happened next wasn't in any of Mr. Denson's predictions. A roar, like a big cat in the jungle, filled the air and the sound of a downshifted Ford rang through the Cutlass. Like a lame Zebra caught in the clutches of the lion, we ducked our head slightly and braced ourselves for what seemed like an eternity, waiting, waiting, waiting…

Finally, I looked back just in time to catch a glimpse of a black on black Ford Galaxy 500 with a man in a straw hat at the helm. It was Old Bruiser and with dear old Dad at the controls! He veered into the oncoming lane and blew past us like we were parked, the force of the event almost sucking poor Garland out from his already precarious position behind the wheel.

"Oh, my gosh. That's my dad!!!!" I said without thinking about the implications of that admission.

"Your dad????" screamed Mr. Denson, suddenly losing all of his composure. "Are you going to drive like him if I let you get your license?" he asked.

"No sir."

His speech turned grim and serious: "Well, Dennis, I know guys like your dad, and we will catch him at the next light. It never pays to speed, boys. You don't really get there any faster." Apparently Mr. Denson had to say that. The code of driver's ed instructors required it.

At the next light we looked and looked but we never did see Dad. I think he was almost in Oklahoma by then, completely disproving the good instructor's theory about how it never pays to speed.

Dad's car could really go. It still lives in legend around the Welch household. Everybody who knew him when he had that thing still talk about it in hushed tones.

Later when he came back to pick me up, I asked him about the garage and the nails.

"Didn't have time to get to that today," he said. I'll bet.

I pressed on: "You didn't happen to pass a little green Cutlass out on Hardy Road today, did you, Dad?"

Realizing he'd been found out, he immediately came clean.

"That was you guys?"

Garland was, I believe, completely traumatized by that event. I'm not sure that he ever drove again.

"Pappy's Christmas" through the years

Patsy, Mandy, and Brian at Mandy's Wedding

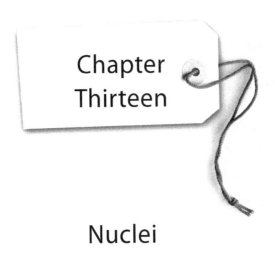

Chapter Thirteen

Nuclei

Call it a clan, call it a network, call it a family.
Whatever you call it, you need one.

Jane Howard

Scientists will tell you that they do not fully understand how protons, neutrons and electrons stay spinning around the nucleus of an atom. Something draws them and keeps them there. If not, everything would just disintegrate and life as we know it would cease to exist. Families are like that. They have these nuclei, people whose personalities are so strong that the family revolves around them and in some cases stay together because of them. Dad was one of those. The Center. His calm and steady hand and powerful personality held it all together. Upon his death the family went through some upheaval, each member dealing with the loss of the nucleus in his or her own way.

DENNIS WELCH

I struggled mightily to hang on. For the next two years I had every kind of physical ailment known to man-all associated with stress. I finally wound up one night in the local emergency room because I was having trouble breathing. The doctor said, "Well, you're lucky. You have only pulled a muscle in the chest area and it is constricting your breathing. If you were 45 you'd be having a heart attack. You've got to calm down."

But, I just couldn't. It took many years for me to fully recover, and all of the mountains of grief came crashing down on me one night in the recording studio. I had gotten married in 1980 to Susie Kline, an incredibly beautiful woman who I met on a blind date. I had already recorded my first album, *Face to Face*, in 1980. It had received extensive airplay in Texas and I eventually signed a record deal with a small independent company out of New Jersey. I was all set to record a nine song record called *Man of Steel*, a mostly power rock album with the occasional ballad sprinkled in for good measure.

About two years after Dad died, I had a most unusual dream. I was sitting in a cafeteria-in fact my old high school cafeteria-and someone came in to tell me that my dad was outside waiting for me. I got up and walked through the doors of the cafeteria and found myself in a strange land. A little house, simple and wooden, stood before me and sure enough there was Dad walking toward me.

His voice was resonant and clear. He got right to the point: "Hello, son. I've been worried about you. You have been grieving now for years and you need to know what's really going on so you can get on with your life."

He turned and began walking slowly toward his house, pausing along the way and waving for me to come along with him. Once inside his little place he gave me the grand tour, which turned out to

158

be not so grand, but it was exactly the kind of place he would have chosen: plainly colored walls, no modern conveniences, very few pictures, simple furniture. He was patient, taking the time to point out every room and hallway.

Then, we walked outside. There, tied up to a small pier directly behind his house, was a little rowboat with a tackle box and fishing poles. "I fish every day," he said. "The weather here is beautiful, and I feel better than ever. My life is good."

My eyes moved out across the little inlet to a vast body of water that appeared to be reflecting the sun's rays. They were so bright that I could hardly take it in without turning away.

"And, what is that out there, Dad?" I asked, speaking for the first time. "That's the Crystal Sea." He looked longingly at it with that laser like stare I remembered so well. "Sometimes I go out there and row around and do a little casting. It's beautiful and bright. Mostly, though, I stay in my little area here behind the house, and I catch all the fish I can handle."

Then, it was time for me to go. He had one last bit of fatherly admonition for me: "Get on with your life, son. Please, do that for me."

And, just like that, he was gone and I was waking up. I got out of bed and wrote a very brief song about that little visit. It's called "The Crystal Sea." It says:

Late at night I almost see him rising in the great beyond.

And walking to the boat he docks behind his house in a lazy pond.

And after he rows awhile I see him fishing in the Crystal Sea.

I took the song to my producer and he insisted that it be the final song on Man of Steel, the closer to a very philosophical and oftentimes esoteric collection of original rock songs. On the night I was to record the vocals I brought along a picture of my dad holding up a stringer of fish, thinking that would inspire me. I had never heard the track, a beautifully orchestrated piece that was moving all by itself without the lyrics. I put on the headphones and prepared to hear the track for the first time. Just at that moment, Paul Mills, the engineer, came into the studio and took my dad's fishing picture off of the music stand and said "maybe later..."

The track began and I began to sing, very clinically, admonishing between the verses to "turn up the guitar" and "please give me more strings." I remember those admonitions because that take was the only take I ever did all the way through. Wherever those master tapes are they still have that between-verses banter. After that rough run through, Paul returned my picture of Dad and his fish and I set it on the music stand so I could see it while I sung. I started the second take...and then fell into uncontrollable sobbing that lasted for almost an hour. I sat down all alone in the semi-darkened studio and wailed. I was heartbroken and I had been for a very long time. This was the moment to let it all out.

When I finished, I walked out of that studio and took my dad's advice. I got on with my life. I began for the first time in many years to enjoy the little things. Susie and I took a few short trips to the hill country of Texas and had a terrific time. In 1985 we had a son, Daniel, and in 1987 we had another son, Dylan. They were and continue to be the absolute lights of my life. My only regret- that Dad never got to meet them. He would have loved them dearly, I'm sure. Sometimes, they act just like him and have some of his mannerisms. Genetics are strong...

Hit men

During the interviews for this book I joked with Patsy that the only thing missing from the story was a hit man. "We had hit men," she said without batting an eyelash. "We sure did."

Then she told me the story about a lady I knew, a mild mannered lady who Mom met in one of her home Bible studies. We'll call her Mary. Mostly a quiet and demure person, Mary was fairly non-descript and not a person you would notice in a crowd, especially this mostly boisterous crowd at Thornton Street. I've always heard that you have to watch out for the quiet ones. That generalization turned out to be true in this case.

She had a son and a daughter. Her daughter married a guy who obviously didn't get along with his mother-in-law. After a few years, they had a couple of kids, Mary's grandkids, whom she loved and adored. One gray afternoon, tragedy struck. Her daughter was killed in a horrible car accident. That alone should have been enough to destroy her, but there was more bad news. The husband decided after her death that Mary could no longer see the children.

Sadly, this kind of thing happens all over America every day. People respond to their basest emotions, and make decisions that negatively impact many future generations. The anger is ratcheted up and sometimes people get physically hurt or killed because of it.

Everybody cranks up the anger, accusations and rhetoric, until somebody get a little crazy. Maybe a lot crazy.

Pushed by her circumstances and anger, Mary slipped over the edge, conjured up a plan, hatched in secret and steeped in revenge. She would hire a hit man and have her son-in-law knocked off. It was a crazy idea, but she was dead serious.

One day, a few days before she had a chance to carry out this little scheme, she came by to see Patsy, and wound up going with her to visit some of their old friends from Thornton Street Baptist Church. By this time, Patsy had been through plenty of turmoil with her own family and had not only come through unscathed, but blessed beyond anything she could have imagined. As the group gathered over coffee and tea, Mary blurted out: "Please, pray for me. I'm about to hire a professional killer and have my son- in-law knocked off. I'm also spending all of my life's savings on attorneys to try and get visitation rights to my grandkids. It's killing me, and I know that what I'm doing isn't right."

Well, I'm pretty sure that ranked right up there with the strangest prayer requests on record. It certainly put a pall over the tea party.

After a brief silence, one of the ladies spoke. "Tell her what you went through, Patsy."

As Patsy began to tell the story about what had happened in her life after Ron's death, a hush fell over the room and everybody leaned forward. Somewhere in Patsy's story was Mary's answer.

Splitting the Atom

After Ron's death, Patsy went through a time of private grieving. The one and only extended time of stability in her life was over. The one man who stayed and loved her and her children and helped her carve out a safe and stable life was gone. Yet, as far as I know she shared her grief or sense of panic with no one. I would never have known that she was wounded except for a single incident that happened quite by accident sometime in the month or so after his passing. I went out on a date, and returned almost immediately because I forgot something. I walked into my house and there she sat in the middle of the floor, surrounded by pictures of Ron and the rest of the family. She had been crying.

Beyond that single moment, I never saw the wheels of her life rattle at all. She returned in earnest to her beloved home Bible studies and to teaching Sunday school in the church she and Ron had been attending for years.

She continued to have miracles in her life. When Ron died, his life insurance amounted to the equivalent of two years of his pay. Not exactly retirement money or anything, but definitely much needed in light of the funeral and medical expenses he had incurred. Unfortunately, ARCO lost the check for six months, finally re-cutting and sending another check in its place. In what I would call an unprecedented move, ARCO asked Patsy's bank to pay her the six months interest she would have earned if she had gotten the money on time.

They agreed. I've never heard of anything like that. The bank certainly wasn't liable for ARCO's mistake, but, as often happens for Patsy, it somehow all worked out for her. She is a wizard when it comes to money- how to save it, how to spend wisely, and how to have enough to give some away to those in need. No financial counselor would believe it, but she has lived since 1978 on just those two years of Ron's pay, and the interest it has earned. She has had some relatively small financial up-ticks and unexpected windfalls along the way, but mostly she has lived frugally while maintaining a very comfortable lifestyle.

Ron would be thrilled that she has been ok in his absence. He would also be okay with knowing his family went through an unsteady time. That's normal. That's what says you were here and that you made a difference. It's the reason grief was invented. If nobody grieves when you die, it's a sure sign that nobody cares.

Upheaval

Everybody in the family had a different reaction to Ron's sickness and death, but it is easy to see now that our reactions were predictable if only one looks deep enough.

Keith reacted to Ron's last days by doing what he did best in a crisis. He leapt in to save the day. He calmly picked out Ron's casket, deciding that "Dad would like this bronze number, because it's about the same color as his new truck." It is fascinating to me that of all of the family, Keith appeared to arrive first at that place you have to get to when you know that someone you love is dying. While everybody else was stalled in the disbelief/denial phase, Keith had jumped directly to acceptance. This is the same guy who, when he heard that Ron was in Methodist Hospital in the Medical Center went directly down to see him. When told he wouldn't be able to visit with Ron at that exact moment, he went outside, climbed in his bucket truck and somehow maneuvered himself up to Ron's second floor window. This was just so he could wave at the man and say hello. That one event described his almost co-dependency with Ron. He couldn't stand to be forced to stay away from him, so he took matters into his own hands and saw him anyway.

Keith also came by the house once a week and mowed and edged the yard. One time Patsy pointed out that the yard didn't necessarily need to be edged every week. His retort said it all: "Dad does it that way. It has to be like that." And "like that" it was.

So, picking the burial plot and the casket was his way of dealing with it. At least for that moment, it seemed to calm him.

Michael was stoic and silent. No tears, really. I'm not sure that he was ever close enough to Ron to feel the kind of connection that Keith or I felt. I'm sure he was hurt, but I'm not sure I ever heard him talk about it.

Patsy held on for the rest of the family's sake. She felt like she needed to be strong for me and the rest of the devastated folks in Ron's clan.

Beverly and Cheryl seemed more affected than almost anyone in the family or extended family. They still cry when they talk about him. Just the other night I did a gig at a little club here in Houston. Mandy's parents, Cheryl and Buddy came to the show, and after it was over she said "I saw a lot of your dad in your performance tonight. I actually felt his presence. I think he'd be proud." Her eyes glistened with emotion as she spoke of him. It has been almost 30 years since he passed away and still he elicits that kind of reaction from almost everyone who knew him.

Another Nucleus-Pappy

Almost immediately after Ron's death, there were other big and mostly unexpected changes in Patsy's family. Keith and wife # 2 (Cheryl) divorced after the birth of their daughter, and she remarried. Beverly married Charlie who began raising Brian as his own son. Michael and Debbie divorced and Michael remained in Germany while Timmy, Ronnie, Randy and Faith came back to the states with their mom. Timmy would eventually move in with Patsy while he finished high school. She took him in and helped him finish school. That wasn't the only school he finished. There is an unwritten rule about Patsy's house: if you stay there, you have to hear about Jesus, and the Bible, and how you should live. You have to. And, you'll be better for it. So Tim got the benefit of her instruction and graduated from her "school of theology" with honors. He thought he was just finishing high school. He will tell you today that staying with "Pappy"-as the younger kids all call her- probably saved him from a heap of trouble and the usual teenage craziness. Though he didn't know it when he got there, he needed stability and direction. He found it there. He will tell you today that the stay at Pappy's was a Godsend.

His brother, Ronnie, also stayed with Pappy for awhile. She almost single-handedly helped him get the last couple of credits so he too could finish high school. He needed guidance and direction and discipline. He found it at Pappy's.

See a pattern here? Life is about choices. Bad things are going to happen and nobody can predict when or where those events will occur. We can't control that. Only God can. But, we can control our reaction to those events. We can turn them into something productive, a life lesson that shapes the outcome and result. Too many times, people react in anger or violence and turn an already bad situation into a completely hopeless one. Patsy used her understanding of the life of Jesus and his teachings to parlay the disarray in her family into something beautiful. She could have panicked, and in her panic, lashed out and perhaps acted in anger or frustration. Instead, she turned the other cheek, loved her neighbor as herself, forgave and forgot any wrongdoing, opened her life and her home to the family, and made herself available for every situation. This was a big test for Patsy and her faith.

There's no point in saying you believe something if you're not going to act upon it. So, no petty feelings or pity parties for Patsy. Okay. This is what we have. Let's make something good out of it.

Perhaps the greatest example of this involved Mandy, Keith's second child. After Cheryl and Keith divorced, Cheryl did what every good parent would have done-she closed ranks around her daughter, protecting her from Keith and his sometimes dangerous lifestyle. She remarried, to a wonderful man, Buddy. They began to raise Mandy in a peaceful home, on a few acres of land in Bellville, many miles from the hustle and bustle of Houston. Cheryl determined to one day tell Mandy the story about Keith and his family, but she was a baby when they divorced and the timing didn't seem right.

Cheryl kindly arranged for Patsy to have regular visits with Mandy after the divorce, so she would drive out to Bellville on weekends and spend time with her. At the time Mandy was blissfully unaware of the true identity of this lady who came to see her on weekends, but she felt a strong bond with her, looked forward to her visits, and always seemed very glad to see her.

Patsy could have been wounded because she couldn't reveal her identity to her own granddaughter. She could have demanded her rights, and taken matters into her own hands. Instead she respected Cheryl and Buddy's decision and abided by their wishes. For years she patiently sat on the porch in Bellville with this little girl and made the most out of her time with her. In time, Cheryl would tell her about this woman, and reveal to her that Patsy was her grandmother, and that Keith was her biological father. Cheryl's wise decision to keep her from Keith had another consequence, perhaps unintended- it probably helped to insure the reconciliation that happened towards the end of his life. If she had been allowed to see Keith at his worst, it might have scarred her in some way and maybe permanently damaged the relationship. Instead, she visited him when he had settled down and was in his right mind and sober. Cheryl was right to handle it the way she did.

The point is that taking the high road paid huge dividends for Patsy and everybody involved. She not only has a great relationship today with Mandy, but a deep and abiding love for Buddy and Cheryl, and vice versa.

Pappy's Christmas

Patsy was determined to maintain the stability she had found and build even stronger bridges to the kinfolk, wives, ex-wives, children, grandchildren, surrogate grandchildren, adopted sons and daughters. It was in that spirit that she began a great family tradition that I believe will continue long after she is gone. "Pappy's Christmas" began almost 30 years ago when she decided to invite all the ex-wives and husbands and grandchildren over to her home the Saturday before Christmas to celebrate the birth of Jesus. In the beginning, it was a very small group. Over the years the families have grown, both in size and in love with each other. These days, space at Pappy's house is not a problem because she has moved to some very nice senior housing out on the north side of town in The Woodlands, Texas. She's older now, and she tires a little easier. Occasionally she'll talk about not doing it anymore but the younger members of the family will have none of that. These gettogethers mean a great deal to them all. There is peace there, and love, and Christmas spirit, and more.

The meals at these shindigs are, well, unusual. Mom has never claimed to be a gourmet cook. In fact, for a long time she put cinnamon in the gravy because she thought that's what made it turn brown. I always thought the gravy tasted a little funny, but it took a trip to Pappy's kitchen from none other than Boots to discover her secret recipe for gravy. "Oh my God'" shouted Boots. "Patsy, this is Cinnamon!" Another time Patsy went through a spell of some kind where she left the plastic bag of giblets in the Thanksgiving turkey WHILE SHE COOKED IT. This went on for several years, the same scenario repeating itself: Turkey in the oven, the more-than-likely carcinogenic odor of melting plastic, shrieks from the other room, carving the bag and the affected section out of the middle of the bird, being thankful, doing it all again the next year.

Sometimes she made pie, which was also an exercise fraught with danger. I walked in one time just in time to see her scraping a smoking heap of cherry and apple pie fragments from the bar into a pot. She shrugged her shoulders and informed me that "They fell off the pan I had up here and landed on top of the bar below. I'm putting it all in a pot and calling it cobbler." It was good cobbler, actually.

See, there's that attitude again…instead of crying over spilled pie, she made a great cobbler out of it. Even her weird cooking adventures teach lessons.

Anyway, the fare at the first installment of Pappy's Christmas was something called "Pile-On." She learned about this dish from Boots. It is fairly easy to prepare. It's sort of like Frito pie but with plain Doritos as the first layer. Then the next layers consist of cheese, then meat, then beans, then lettuce, then tomatoes, and finally a couple of spoonfuls of salsa. Sometimes we consider changing the menu, but that is quickly shot down. Pile-on has become synonymous with Pappy's Christmas. It is comfort food with a capital C. In fact, if I eat pile-on at anytime during the rest of the year, I feel like Santa Claus will show up at any moment.

The crowds at Pappy's Christmas include all of the ex-wives and current wives and husbands, all of the grandchildren, great grandchildren, surrogate grandchildren, in-laws, outlaws, and even people who are not in her family but wish they were. One of these individuals, Aubrey Karr, swears he's related, and every time the subject comes up he whips out a table napkin and begins drawing his version of Patsy and Ronald's family tree. His tree somehow ends up with him being a cousin of mine. He even calls me "Cuz" when he sees me. So, we've adopted him and his wife Janet, and their kids. They are as close as any of the kinfolk.

Patsy has a lot of people looking out for her. When her house flooded during tropical storm Allison, it was Beverly's husband Charlie that drove the 30 or so miles through several feet of water to rescue her. When something is going on at her church, my "Cuz" and his wife come and get her so she doesn't have to drive at night. Brian and his family come by to see her often, usually bringing supper with them so she won't have to cook. Faith and her family drive over from Bridge City, Texas and spend the night from time to time, and call several times a week to see about her. Tim calls from Germany at least once a week, and emails more often than that. Until recently, Rosie mowed her lawn and my kids help her with her technology issues and around the house maintenance. Cheryl and her husband take her to special events and plays. Mandy calls often and visits with her from time to time. Her friends and Bible students call several times a week and drop over.

And then sometimes, it seems like she has angels. Patsy recently moved from her house on Hummingbird Lane out to The Woodlands, Texas. Even that experience is a story all by itself.

For some time she had felt that a house was just too much for her to keep up with. The aging house, the oversized yard, all of it was becoming more than she (and we) could handle. After a lot of thought and prayer, she decided she would sell the last house her and Ron ever lived in together.

When she and Ron first moved to 407 Hummingbird Lane, it was out in the country, with a meadow behind her back fence where the neighbor kids raised a few sheep and other farm animals for their FFA projects. By the time she decided to move to the Woodlands, that serene setting had been replaced by a dusty field of thundering construction trucks and equipment kicking up dust and making racket from before sunup until after dark every day. They even had a helicopter that buzzed around and landed from time to time.

My father-in-law, Al Kline, came up with an idea for Mom that turned out to be providential. He suggested that Mom go over to the construction company and ask if they might be interested in buying her place, perhaps to expand their operations and to have more office space. But before she could make the trek over to the offices, she casually mentioned his idea to Charlie, Beverly's husband. "My brother hunts with that guy," said Charlie. "Let me contact him and let him know what you're doing."

So, the owner of the construction company stopped by Mom's place one morning and sat and talked with her about the home and what her plans were. "Mrs. Welch, how much do you want for the house?" he asked her. She named a fair price, and he accepted her offer on the spot. No repairs needed to be made, no allowance for issues the house might have, nothing. He just paid what she wanted for the home.

When it came time to close on the house, I went to the closing with her, and the construction company sent their CFO. After all the papers were signed and before we left, the CFO said "you know, I'm not really a religious man, but I have to tell you that all of this whole process had moments that seemed almost like they were planned out somehow. For example, me and the owner came down Hummingbird Lane two weeks before we ever even knew this house was for sale, and sat directly in front of your place, Mrs. Welch, and talked about how great it would be if we could get one or two of these houses to expand our operation."

Then, one of your relatives who hunts with us called and casually mentioned that you might want to sell, and it turned out to be the EXACT SAME HOUSE WE HAD LOOKED AT AND SAT IN FRONT OF ONLY WEEKS BEFORE. Very unusual, I would say, wouldn't you?"

It was about to get a little stranger. This man had been kind enough to go by the house on Hummingbird Lane and take down some curtains Mom had been unable to extricate from the wall and bring them with him. She had borrowed those curtains from Beverly and Charlie some time back and she wanted to return them as soon as possible. After all the papers were signed, I said, "Mom, let's wait till tomorrow to take these curtains back out to Roman Forest (where Beverly and Charlie live). It's kind of late, and I can do that for you tomorrow."

"Roman Forest?" the CFO asked. "Well, I live in Roman Forest." "Yes," Mom said, "But you probably don't live near our family out there, The Tanners."

"The Tanners?" the now obviously stunned CFO asked incredulously. "You mean the guy that has the really cool orange 57 Chevy? Those Tanners? Why, they're my nearest neighbors."

Mom got her check, and we all headed out to our cars to leave. After she and I got into her car I said, "Mother, you have the most unusual life. These guys bought your house for exactly your asking price, they took down your curtains for you, and now they're even going to deliver them. Amazing."

Her life is like that, filled with surprises and friends and family, activities and joy. She may live to be a hundred, but already the end of her days are better than the beginning. She hardly has any time to herself. You would think that she'd be slowing down by now, that her calendar would start thinning out a bit, like many so called "Golden Agers." Not Patsy. She's busier than ever.

I always am amazed at the turnout and enthusiasm at Pappy's Christmas. I am just as astounded when I drop by her house for coffee or lunch and the phone never stops ringing and people just drop by unannounced, just to say hello and check on her. I never experience these moments without thinking that this could have all turned out different. She could have acted out of fear, hired a lawyer or a hit man, and slugged it out until she "won".

Instead she made "cobbler" out of it.

By the way, Mary never hired her hit man, either. She heard Patsy's story, decided to take another route, a higher road that required supernatural doses of humility and kindness. She fired all but one of her battery of lawyers and began praying for her son-in-law instead of conspiring to kill him. Miraculously, the judge in her case had a complete change of heart and decreed that she should have all the visitation rights available to her. A peaceful solution was found and everybody prospered.

A Patsy Moment - Driving Miss Patsy

I have this great little VHS tape of Patsy and Boots sitting on a couch and recounting all the crazy years together as friends. There are hundreds of funny stories, but almost every other one involves Patsy's driving escapades. Officer Pete did not know what he was unleashing on the world back there when he gave Patsy her license. He couldn't have known that her guardian angels (and mine, and anyone else who ever rode with her) would have to work overtime.

There was the one where she was at the grocery store and, after finishing her shopping, she decided to just go forward instead of backing out of her parking space. Unfortunately, there was a large cement divider in front of her car, so when she climbed up on it, she got stuck. She got out of her car and asked an obviously stunned but still witty man which way she should go. "I don't think it makes a hell of a lot of difference, ma'am." She went on forward and dragged off her mufflers in the process.

Then, there's the one when she turned in the Welch mansion driveway, waved hello to Dad and Michael and then proceeded to drive directly through the back of the garage WITHOUT HITTING A BRAKE. Even once. Keith was riding with her. He got out, ran around to the back of the garage and announced "hey, you can see the back yard from in here!!!"

Or perhaps you'd like to hear about the time she took a wrong turn onto a new highway being constructed and somehow made her way down to where the pavers and other highway building types were working. "How would you suggest I get out of here?" she queried to the wide eyed construction crew. "Well ma'am," one of the gents began, "I'm not sure how you get out of here, but I would love to hear how you got down here in the first place." She wasn't sure.

"We're gonna die, Dennis! Pray!" That was her regular admonition every time she drove me anywhere that required us to enter the freeway. She would come to a complete stop on the entrance ramp (I know, these are the people you cuss, right?), then she would gun it, her 65 Ford Falcon with the tiny whining, wheezing, un-powerful, plastic-sounding excuse for an engine. Twenty, thirty, forty…other cars were whizzing by at seventy and eighty. My life flashed before my eyes and sometimes I would scream out in terror. We always made it. She's never had a wreck that was her fault.

Angels, man. I'm telling you they are real.

One time, she and Boots were visiting my uncles at their house on Homestead. Homestead had recently been widened because it was a growing area and the traffic had increased dramatically. "When you back out of here, Patsy, you're gonna have to gun it!" Boots commanded. Somehow, the "gun it" part of that sentence is all Patsy heard, and so, while everyone was still visiting and calmly finishing up their conversation with the engine gently idling, Patsy rammed it in reverse and floored it. My relatives were in mid sentence when suddenly her vehicle burned rubber and left Uncle Jimmy's driveway and leapt across Homestead and over the grass median and into the neighbor's driveway across the street, barely missing their garage by, as Boots says, "one coat of paint." My stunned relatives stood agape.

They soon learned that this is just how Patsy drives. Years later when this kind of thing would happen, they would ignore it completely and continue to talk among themselves as if nothing at all had transpired.

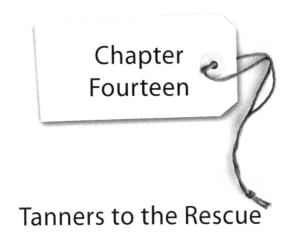

Chapter Fourteen

Tanners to the Rescue

…A man reaps what he sows."

St. Paul, Galatians 6:7 (NIV)

Miracles.

You know they happen, and sometimes they have even happened to you. But, if it's been a while since you've seen one, it's easy to forget that they're possible.

One Sunday, just this year, I saw one with my own eyes, and I am eternally grateful. Patsy, a tad above four score years old was living alone at the time in her little one-bedroom apartment in The Woodlands, Texas.

She had stopped driving a few years before of her own volition. It happened without a lot of fanfare or handwringing. One day, she and I were at the Target store near her home, and I asked her to take me for a spin around the parking lot in her car. She had told me several times

177

recently that she had been struggling some when she drove, but had never been specific about what the issues were.

So, we took a little drive. When she was finished, she wheeled her little maroon Hyundai into a parking space with all the ease of a veteran wheelman with no obvious issues whatsoever. We turned the car off and I asked "Mom, why are you afraid to drive? That was terrific!"

And, then she did us all a big favor, the kind of favor that all elderly people should give their kids, but many alas, do not. She said "Son, I know HOW to drive a car. That's not my problem. My problem is decision making. If there are too many choices, I get confused. And, I'm afraid I am going to hurt someone someday."

And, with that, she handed me her keys and after more than half a century of being the captain of her own ship, she relinquished command without a single whimper or complaint. That brave decision meant that others would have to pick her up to go shopping or take her to church, or run errands with or for her. As expected, her family and friends lined up to do just that, happy to help her out whenever she needed it.

That decision-to get out from behind the wheel- was a tough one for her. Remember that from a very early age, she had been on her own, making her own decisions, fending for herself. She was one of the most independent people I have ever known. And, in spite of her many friends and huge social circle, she was also one of the most private.

But, the decision to stop driving may have saved her life and extended it in a way that she could not have imagined at the time.

Falling

After Susie and I moved to Austin a few years ago, Brian and Connie and their four daughters became the geographically closest family members to mom, and we were thankful. They happily joined the list of family and friends who did her grocery shopping. They took her to church anytime that she wanted to go. Their oldest daughter, Emily, worked at a pizza parlor nearby, and she would just drop by out of the blue and visit with mom and bring her favorite pizza.

Then, one Sunday morning just a very few months ago, Brian and his youngest daughter, Elizabeth (Lizzie), dropped by to pick her up for church, and they knocked on her door several times with no response. After a few more attempts, Brian began to worry and started thinking about how to break her door down. But, he was hesitant, not because he couldn't do it. He is a strong young man who could have easily kicked her door in with plenty to spare. But, he was afraid that if she was sleeping that the episode might scare her and he didn't want to risk that.

Remember that for later in this miracle story. Brian is a tender hearted good man who really loves his grandmother, and his decision not to kick her door in and startle her was just one of a long list of really good deeds he was about to do for her on this day and in the days to come.

We got in touch with the maintenance man at mom's apartments and while Brian and Lizzie were waiting on him to show up, a fireman magically appeared, and then a man with the master keys showed up to let them in.

When they got inside, they found mom lying beside her bed unable to get up. She had passed out during the night and had fallen next to her bed and was too weak to call anyone for help. Brian and

Lizzie quickly called 9-1-1 and mom was whisked off to the hospital just in the nick of time. Susie and I raced down to Houston to be by her side. When we arrived, she was in the ER,, relatively lucid and talking a blue streak to anyone who would listen. The doctor reassured us all that she would be fine, and they went to work on figuring out what caused this scary episode.

We all sat down in the waiting room, and then….it happened. "The Magnolia Miracle".

Maybe...

We've probably all had events in our life that are somehow cauterized, cast in stone, bronzed to sit on our memories' shelves so that we can revisit them forever. This was one of those moments, an act of profound unselfishness and gratitude.

We had hardly found our seats in the waiting room when Connie began the conversation: "Brian and I would like to talk with you about maybe having Pappy move in with us. How would you feel about that?"

Her reasoning was sound. Mom has a ton of friends and family and they all live in the Houston area for the most part. If Susie and I were to take her back to Austin to live (which we would have been happy to do), she would lose touch with a lot of her social circle, and frankly, she needed that interaction, especially now.

But wait. Connie and Brian are raising four daughters, and are homeschooling three of them now as the oldest starts college. How in the world will they do this?

I asked what anyone would ask: "Are you sure?"

Their strong answer came without any hesitation: "We're POSITIVE."

We thanked them and then went off to ponder and pray about their offer.

In a few weeks, mom was out of the hospital and in a rehab facility and making some good progress. One night, Brian and Connie and Susie and I went out to dinner to discuss what might be next for mom. There was no waffling, no backpedaling, no question in their minds what was next. Nothing had changed.

We asked again: "Are you sure?"

Yes. They were, and I guess I already knew that. Brian reassured us that this was not something they had only recently considered. He had been thinking about it for years, and his mind had been made up long before this crisis.

Then, Connie asked Brian to tell us about a paper he had written in elementary school about what he would do if he had a million dollars. His answer (even back then)? He would build a big house and take his grandmother in to live with him.

So, he had been thinking about this move for her for his whole life. Enough said. If we could talk her into it, this was the right move in every way.

I sat down with mom and started the conversation. It's important, I think, to remember that elderly people are still people. They've accomplished a lot in their lives as a rule, and they're not idiots or children who need to be admonished or talked down to. Mom was having some cognitive issues, but she understood that going back to her little apartment to live alone was not going to be one of her options.

It helped in a way that she had stayed a few days in a rehab facility, an institution that housed a lot of elderly patients, who, like her, were struggling in one way or the other. She saw that scenario firsthand, and it was easy for me to offer the comparison so that she could make the right decision: *Mom, do you want strangers around you or do you want people who love you to be there when you need them?*

That turned out to be one of our shortest conversations.

Within just a few days construction began on a beautiful room, built just for mom and attached to the Tanner house in a way that would be best for her and what would likely be a throng of visitors that were sure to be there once she got settled.

While construction was going on, she moved into a little guest area in the back of the house that had a twin bed and an area they set up just for her. It was beautiful, really. The family was so conscientious about what she wanted and needed. When her room was finished, they installed a nice flat screen TV, and hung all of her favorite pictures. Photos of the family line her shelves. A large black and white photo of her and dad sits directly in front of her bed. Dad is smiling, beaming actually. She always talks about that picture, and how happy they both look. She misses him terribly, and I would guess that he will be the first person she looks for when she gets to Heaven. After Jesus greets her with a hug and a hello, and a "well done", Dad will be next. He is probably impatiently tapping his toe, awaiting the moment.

Every now and then, mom will ask me "Why are these people doing this? Why are they being so kind to me?"

And, my answer is always the same. "We reap what we sow, right mom? You sowed kindness and love instead of anger and discord, and this is what happens."

Miracles. Love. Sacrifice. Yes, it's difficult sometimes. But, for the most part, it is unspeakable joy for both mom and the Tanners. Connie cooks her meals and takes care of her every need. The kids all help out, too. Each has their assignment, and they all-Emily, Madelyn, Courtney, and Lizzie-carry them out with love. Her former daughter in laws, Beverly and Cheryl, are also there to fill in the gaps when needed.

When I'm there and I'm watching all the activity I often think of all the families that are torn to pieces because they couldn't figure out how to just let things go, to forgive, to reach out, to take positive steps toward building great relationships. Instead, they let the waves of anger and divisiveness drive them up on the rocks and there they remain.

Throughout her life, mom certainly had every opportunity to do just that-to mope, to carry a grudge, to wallow in self-pity about her circumstances. Instead, she did something else. And, now, her grandson and his family are repaying her every single day, far beyond what she could ever expect.

More riches. The kind that cannot be explained or deposited into a bank account. She's still receiving the benefits of a life well-lived, from making decisions based not on what she felt at the time, but on what was right for everybody concerned.

Spend just a little bit of time at The Tanner Mansion, and you'll see that her barns are filled to excess with blessings. "The Pappy Team" is going full speed. Connie runs the show on the ground there. Susie keeps up with all of her medical and insurance needs and issues. One of the Tanner girls wakes her up every morning and sits with her while she sips her coffee and relishes the visit with her great granddaughter.

Brian comes home from his job many evenings and takes his dinner into her room to dine with her to be sure she eats.

She is loved. She is waited on hand and foot. Her every need is met by people who volunteer to do so. She is one of the lucky ones, the blessed, and on most days she is well aware of it.

It has been a tough year. She has spiraled down physically and mentally, taking a horrendous fall in the summer that she has not yet recovered from. Boots has passed away, and that, as expected, has hit her very hard. She almost didn't go to the funeral, but decided to at the last minute. "No one will really care if I come to it or not," she said. "But if I don't go, Boots will talk about it forever when I get to Heaven. So, I guess I'd better try." When she arrived at the chapel, there in the foyer, was an oversize picture of her and Boots, standing out beside Mom's house, probably taken right before they headed out on one mission trip or another.

She is feeble, and when she arrived at the service, practically the entire room stood and came over to her, thronging her and covering her with hugs and kisses and hello's. Her heart was broken over the loss of her lifelong friend, but she stood bravely, and as always, was a great example to the people around her who love and admire her so. Once again, maybe for the last time, they leaned on her for support in a difficult time.

Someday, maybe soon, she will finish her work here and go on to what's next. She will leave knowing assuredly that her latter days were better than her first. To think: She started her life out with almost no one wanting her, and she'll end her life being loved by so many.

Napkin from Pre-Funeral Celebration

Chapter Fifteen

Testify

Ordinary riches can be stolen. Real riches cannot. In your soul are infinitely precious things that cannot be taken from you.

Oscar Wilde

One after another they came to the podium that day at the "prefuneral celebration." All day they walked boldly up in front of a crowd of friends and strangers and spilled their guts about what their lives had been like when Patsy and Boots had shown up. No soft selling, no glossing over the bad parts.

These were real people with real problems and they actually considered it a great privilege to recount their stories. They were moving and honest, and they reminded me over and over again that special day about what I believe and why I believe it.

For example, it reminded me that Grace is what we get when we don't necessarily deserve it. And, that Humility is the ability to go back anytime we want, to that place in our lives where we had very little to offer and our hearts were heavy and almost defeated. Arrogance is the opposite of humility. It is dishonest, a lie we tell ourselves over and over again until we actually believe it. The lie? That we are not needy and we never have been...

As I watched these brave and sometimes eloquent souls tell their tales I couldn't help but think of the Apostle Paul and his dramatic conversion. Remember that story? He was struck down on the road to Damascus, temporarily blinded by the sheer magnitude, beauty and glory of God. He had to stay that way for three days until Ananias, an obedient servant of God went to him and laid hands on him so he could see again. Saul was a fire breathing, Christian-hating enemy of the early Church. He struck fear into the hearts of people everywhere he went, and he had even killed individuals who had the audacity to believe in this so called Messiah. God looked at Saul and saw something He could use. He looked past the murderer that he was and saw the man he could become.

My guess is that Saul's conversion was so dramatic that he could go back there in his mind and heart, and, anytime he wanted, he could literally feel the scales on his eyes, and the helplessness he endured until obedient Ananias showed up. Throughout Paul's life and all that he accomplished, this one event probably kept him from becoming arrogant. His conversion story also taught the early church a vital lesson. Nobody is beyond God's unlimited ability to help.

In some ways, his story is like Patsy's. Obedient people showed up in her life, too, in spite of the hassle and the fear of what people would say: JD, Lillian, Boots, pastors, friends, and relatives. They could have ignored her, castigated her, clucked their tongues like the Pharisees and thanked God and their lucky stars that they weren't like her. They could have avoided her house like the plague and waited for her to "snap out of it" and "grow up" and ...all the things we say about people when we forget who we are and where we came from and how often we have been rescued, revived, and resuscitated. She had many Ananiases in her life. Thank God for them.

Rescuing people is almost always risky. Think about it. Paul was the archenemy of the Church. I can just see Ananias tapping on the phone and asking God: "And you want me to WHAT? Go to him and PRAY for HIM???" I'm sure that Ananias had his doubts. He went anyway.

His declaration after he reaches Paul is simple and beautiful. Acts 9 tells the story: "Ananias went to the house and entered it. Placing his hands on Saul, he said 'Brother Saul, the Lord-Jesus who appeared to you on the road as you were coming here has sent me to you so that you may see again and be filled with the Holy Spirit.'"

No comment from Ananias about what a jerk Saul had been, no subtle reminders about his reputation for being a killer and a jailer of Christ- followers. Saul was a murderer and it didn't even come up in the conversation with Ananias. He called Saul "brother Saul." Wow that had to have stuck in his throat a little as he said it.

Patsy and Boots have been through a lot. They haven't actually committed murder, but don't kid yourself-they thought about it. They'll tell you they did and only the grace of God stopped them. Like Paul they have excellent memories and, like the rest of us, can easily recollect all the shortcomings and mistakes in their lives.

But, more importantly, they can recount with great clarity the day the scales fell off their eyes. That moment lives forever in their hearts. Every time the phone rings and someone is in trouble, they return for just a moment, however briefly, to the day when they were in need...blind, sick, destitute. It instantly appears in their mind's eye like an old photo album and for a heartbeat or two they see again the slightly worn and sepia images of what they once were.

And then, off they go. No second thoughts about their safety; no wor- ries about what the neighbors would think; and no concerns about the time of day or night or how much sleep or money or time they would lose if they answered the call. They simply answer, over and over again, for years and years now, decades even. Out the door, in the car, Bible in hand, food and drink and money and clothes and anything…literally anything that a person could need, they carry with them.

They are sort of spiritual benefactors, quietly going about their work, giving of all they have to those in need.

Just like rich people.

Dennis Welch

Dennis Welch has always been a word guy. From the tender age of four when he learned quite by accident that he could spell, he's loved words and the power of a great sentence and story.

"My mother came home from seeing Santa Claus and she spelled it out for my dad," he says. "Somehow I knew how to interpret that." Dennis would spend a lot of his early years in the school library, reading Mark Twain, E.B. White, and others, learning about the value of a well-crafted tale, and how words can inspire and forever change the way one thinks.

Dennis has contributed short stories, articles, and essays for various publications over the years, but in some ways, this book came as a complete surprise. After interviewing his mom every Saturday morning for a few months, he began writing Rich People Shop Here, thinking that he would just go down to the local office supply and print off copies for the younger relatives in his family. Along the way, a veteran of the publishing business began reading the manuscript and strongly encouraged Dennis to publish it, saying that the book would inspire and encourage people with its message and story.

And so, *Rich People Shop Here* was born. It is Dennis' first book.

Dennis is married to Susie and their family is Sons Daniel and wife Megan, Dylan and wife Kristi. They have four Grandchildren, Alexis, Matthew, Mazy and Alivia.

Susie and Dennis live in Austin, Texas.

Acknowledgements

It would be difficult to thank everyone who has had a hand in making this book come to life. These kinds of projects have many contributors, personal, professional, and financial. There's been a lot of encouragement from a wide range of folks. Anyway, here's my stab at thanking those who helped make Rich People Shop Here go from just a Word document to a real book that we hope has real impact in the world.

First of all I'd like to thank my family and extended family. Mom and Boots, thanks for letting me tell your story and for not just talking the talk, but walking the walk. You're still doing that and seeing it happen changed my life, too, along with all of the people you have impacted. To my father who cannot be here to see this moment, thanks for your example to me about how a man should take care of his family and be a friend. For those who are mentioned in the pages of the book, it is a privilege for me to tell your stories. Thanks for letting me do that. You all have a hand in any lives that are changed or any encouragement or guidance this book gives. You may not know till you get to heaven what all their names are.

To Kay and Al Kline for raising Susie: You did good, and I've been the beneficiary for the past 30 years. She is an amazing wife who has pitched in and encouraged and done everything asked of her so this could all happen. I'm a blessed guy because you bent the twig so beautifully.

To my sons Daniel and Dylan. It has been a privilege to be your father. You have taught me plenty about Love and Mercy, and much of what I learned from you both is in and between the lines of this book.

Barbara Henricks, you will never know what your encouragement meant to me as I wrote the chapters and sent them off to you at your request. Your little "Where is Patsy now?" notes meant you cared. I'm glad you still do. Having you lead the Rich People Shop Here media team is absolutely priceless. I am honored that you care enough to be involved.

To George Gallup, Jr. and his late wife Kinny, thanks so much for writing the foreword to the book. George, I know you miss her terribly. Her kindness and yours to the Welch family will not be forgotten.

To others who have encouraged me: Derek Bell, Terry Whalin, Jennifer Bell, Aubrey and Janet Karr, my sis Darlene, Geoff Brewer, Bob Beaudine, Carolyn Castleberry, and many, many too numerous to mention: Thank You. Your words and advice and everything you did came at just the right time.

It's my privilege to be the messenger.

a Book's Mind

If you'd like Dennis Welch to speak to your group or event contact Susie at: **(512) 506-9725** or email: **Susie@BeArticulate.com**

Whether you want to purchase bulk copies of *Rich People Shop Here,* or buy another book for a friend, get it now at: **www.RichPeopleShopHere.com**.

Do you have a book that you would like to publish? Contact A Book's Mind: info@abooksmind.com. www.abooksmind.com

You may contact Dennis directly at: www.RichPeopleShopHere.com

CPSIA information can be obtained
at www.ICGtesting.com
Printed in the USA
FSHW02n2015110818
51201FS